"Oh, the unbelievable wisdom and insight this woman has into living life successfully. Jan Silvious gives us all the sound biblical principles we need to become Smart Girls. She doesn't miss a trick! When these truths are applied, there's no question that life is going to be a lot more doable and enjoyable. They simply work . . . and isn't that what we're all looking for?"

—Luci Swindoll
Women of Faith® Speaker and Author, *Life! Celebrate It*

"Like Solomon, she is anointed with wisdom from on high. *Smart Girls Think Twice* is the best of Jan Silvious. Buy it, read it, give it to friends, and pray we are all smart enough to walk the paths that take us *around* the maiming minefields that explode into a lifetime of grief."

—Dee Brestin
Author, *The Friendships of Women* and *A Woman of Wisdom*

"Jan's words inspire me to *think twice* about what I'm doing and thinking. She's a smart girl! In fact, anyone who reads this book can be a Smart Girl. I'd call that a smart decision *and* a good deal!"

—Marilyn Meberg
Women of Faith® Speaker and Author, *Love Me Never Leave Me*

"Everyone needs to read this book. It could save you grief and much of the pain that goes with making missteps on your journey. It is pure wisdom straight from the scriptures and totally relevant to all."

—Kay Arthur
Co-CEO, Precept Ministries, International, and Author,
Precept Upon Precept Bible Studies

"Jan Silvious is in a league of her own. In *Smart Girls Think Twice* she delivers powerful and practical insights to how we spend time, money, and words. Jan encourages us to think twice about the attitudes and decisions that impact our relationships and create consequences. Her trademark wit and wisdom leave you inspired, determined, and feeling empowered. C'mon Big Girls . . . it's time to be Smart Girls."

—Ellie Lofaro
Bible Teacher, Author, and Speaker

"After reading Jan Silvious's book, I realize that having sense is not that common. We need God's wisdom to help us sort out things. In *Smart Girls Think Twice* I could actually sense Jan pulling for us. She wants us to do better and to be better. She beautifully exercises her gift as the teacher who enlightens, the counselor who encourages, and the life coach who runs along the sidelines, cheering us on toward the goal. I'm definitely smarter for having read it."

—Babbie Mason
Singer, Songwriter, Author, and TV Talk-Show Host

"*Smart Girls Think Twice* is a wonderful book. Jan Silvious, a model of wisdom for today's Christian woman, gives sound, biblical advice and encouragement for women at all stages of life. Sharing from her heart and rich life experiences, her formula for awkward situations—Is it true? Is it kind? Is it necessary?—is a treasure. Warm, funny, and smart . . . you will love this book."

—Dr. Marie Chapian
Author and Conference Speaker

"Pick me! Pick me! I want to be a Smart Girl! Packed full of practical wisdom, *Smart Girls Think Twice* offers sound biblical counsel, creative steps of action, and hope for better choices in the future. Instead of living defeated lives over poor decisions in the past, we are encouraged in a new way of forward thinking about the choices that go before us. This important book from Jan Sivilous calls for a revisit to integrity-driven decisions while sending out a message loud and clear to my generation of women: our choices hold monumental importance in our lives. *Smart Girls Think Twice* is a must-read for any woman who desires to be a part of the Smart Girl *club*. After reading this book, you will want club membership too!"

—Lisa Whittle
Speaker and Author, *Behind Those Eyes*

"Jan Silvious has done it again! An imminently practical book, *Smart Girls Think Twice* is a wise companion through the terrain of life that matters most—and a hedge against a ton of grief and regret. Give yourself a couple of hours to take in Jan's wisdom and be blessed."

—Paula Rinehart
Author, *Strong Women, Soft Hearts* and *Better Than My Dreams*

smart girls think twice

Making Wise Choices When It Counts

JAN SILVIOUS

THOMAS NELSON
Since 1798

NASHVILLE   DALLAS   MEXICO CITY   RIO DE JANEIRO   BEIJING

Published in Nashville, Tennessee, by Thomas Nelson. Thomas Nelson is a registered trademark of Thomas Nelson, Inc.

Thomas Nelson, Inc. titles may be purchased in bulk for educational, business, fund-raising, or sales promotional use. For information, please e-mail SpecialMarkets@ThomasNelson.com.

Unless otherwise noted, Scripture quotations are taken from the *Holy Bible*, New Living Translation, © 1996, 2004. Used by permission of Tyndale House Publishers, Inc., Wheaton, Illinois 60189. All rights reserved.

Scripture quotations marked KJV are taken from the Holy Bible, King James Version.

Scripture quotations marked MSG are taken from *The Message* by Eugene H. Peterson, © 1993, 1994, 1995, 1996, 2000. Used by permission of NavPress Publishing Group. All rights reserved.

Scripture quotations marked NASB are taken from the New American Standard Bible®, © 1960, 1962, 1963, 1968, 1971, 1972, 1973, 1975, 1977, 1995 by The Lockman Foundation. Used by permission.

Scripture quotations marked NCV are taken from the New Century Version®. © 2005 by Thomas Nelson, Inc. Used by permission. All rights reserved.

Scripture quotations marked NIV are taken from the Holy Bible: New International Version®. © 1973, 1978, 1984 by International Bible Society. Used by permission of Zondervan Publishing House. All rights reserved.

Scripture quotations marked NKJV are taken from the New King James Version®, © 1982 by Thomas Nelson, Inc. Used by permission. All rights reserved.

Library of Congress Cataloging-in-Publication Data

Silvious, Jan, 1944–
  Smart girls think twice : making wise choices when it counts / Jan Silvious.
    p. cm.
Includes bibliographical references.
ISBN 978-0-7852-2815-8 (pbk.)
  1. Christian women—Religious life. 2. Choice (Psychology)—Religious aspects—Christianity.
3. Decision making—Religious aspects—Christianity. I. Title.

BV4527.S447 2007
248.8'43—dc22   2007044357

Printed in the United States of America
08 09 10 11 RRD 7 6 5 4 3 2 1

To my precious family:

We are twelve blessed people to have one another. My heart belongs to each of you in ways only we understand. Your love and support give me wings. I am forever grateful.

To my beloved girlfriends:

You know who you are. You know why we are friends. Truly, "I thank my God in all my remembrance of you" (Phil. 1:3 NASB).

And to the Big Girls who are on this journey with me:

Let's press on with passion as we apply our hearts to *do life* with excellence. May we bring great delight to our heavenly Father as we become Smart Girls who honor Him.

Contents

Contents

Acknowledgments

With heartfelt appreciation to my Smart Girl midwives: Rebecca Price, Debbie Wickwire, Laura Barker, and Carolyn Capp. This Smart Girl baby could not have seen the light of day without each of you!

And to Shirley Sharpe, who made it her righteous business to pray this child into existence, my deep gratitude.

An Intelligent Attitude Toward Life

How did I ever get into this mess?

What was I thinking?

Why does this keep happening to me?

Where do I go from here?

When did life become so complicated?

If you have ever found yourself asking questions like these, you're in good company, dear sister. From time to time, each of us lands in the middle of a situation that leaves us looking back to see where our lives took a wrong turn. And more often than not, if we are honest with ourselves, that wrong turn was the result of making an unwise choice, or even a whole bunch of them.

Each day you and I face countless decisions, opportunities, and challenges. Some are simple: Flats or heels? White or whole wheat?

Plastic or paper? Others deserve a bit more thought: Cash or charge? Do I really need this or do I just want it? Should we paint the house this weekend or kick back and relax? And many choices, perhaps more than we'd like to think, have the power to set our lives on an entirely different course: Shall I continue in my current job, or should I take the risk of starting my own business? Is

> Decision is a risk rooted in the courage of being free.[1]
>
> —PAUL TILLICH

this problem with my child important enough to confront now, or should I wait and see what happens? Do I continue to work at this relationship, or is it time to walk away?

All of these decisions together determine not only where life will take us but also set the mood for our journey. We'll either walk in a cloud of uncertainty and regret or we'll press on confidently, satisfied with our choices and eager to see where they lead us. The difference comes in knowing when we need to think twice about a decision, and that difference is what sets Smart Girls apart from the rest.

This book is all about when and how to think twice so that you can make smart choices and live in that confident zone of security in which you are content with your decisions. A Smart Girl doesn't have to second-guess herself, nor does she live with regrets for what might have been. She approaches vital decisions with an intentional heart and proceeds with a poise that comes only from making a wise choice.

A Smart Girl chooses to *think* smart. It's not a matter of IQ. It's a matter of the heart, a willingness to take that extra look at choices that matter. She doesn't obsessively dwell on a choice. Once she has considered the consequences and made her decision, she moves on.

A Smart Girl knows that mistakes are inevitable. She doesn't look back with self-pity or self-loathing. If she realizes she didn't choose the best option, she acknowledges it and determines to make a better choice the next time. She knows what is . . . *is,* and she moves forward from that point. She will learn from the past but never, ever wallow in it. She knows that perfection is unattainable, so she is content to make the best choice she can based on what she knows and then trust God with the rest.

A Smart Girl shines in her ability to avoid repeating the same mistake twice. She learns from her own experiences as well as from the missteps of others. She also reads with a learner's heart. She approaches the Scriptures, as well as other books of substance, with an ear to listen and an eye to observe.

Sometimes, despite her best efforts and through no fault of her own, a Smart Girl faces situations she didn't see coming. Those unexpected circumstances bring out her well-established God-confidence. Even when she's blindsided by life, she trusts that the Lord will be true to His promise to cause "all things to work together for good to those who love God, to those who are called according to His purpose" (Rom. 8:28 NASB). She allows God to work His purposes without interference.

The Essential Quality of a Smart Girl

There is a rich, multifaceted Hebrew word that encompasses the essence of what it takes to become a Smart Girl. That word is *châkam.* In many places, it is translated as *wisdom,* but the original word, for which we have no English equivalent, embodies *wisdom, knowledge, experience, insight,* and *judgment*—everything we most need to make good choices. Its meaning could be summarized as "an intelligent attitude toward the experiences of life."[2]

The book of Proverbs is full of references to *châkam,* and the following verses reflect why those who have this quality can walk through life with confidence in each choice they make.

Tune your ears to wisdom,
  and concentrate on understanding.
Cry out for insight,
  and ask for understanding.
Search for them as you would for silver;
  seek them like hidden treasures.
Then you will understand what it means to fear the LORD,
  and you will gain knowledge of God.
For the LORD grants wisdom!
  From his mouth come knowledge and understanding.
He grants a treasure of common sense to the honest.
  He is a shield to those who walk with integrity.
He guards the paths of the just
  and protects those who are faithful to him.
Then you will understand what is right, just, and fair,
  and you will find the right way to go.
For wisdom will enter your heart,
  and knowledge will fill you with joy.
Wise choices will watch over you.
  Understanding will keep you safe. (2:2–11)

Don't you love that passage? Oh, the inexpressible comfort of having "an intelligent attitude toward life." That is the mark of a Smart Girl; that is *châkam*.

How Smart Girls Get That Way

Making good choices isn't natural in our fallen human condition, but each of us can develop this skill by learning and mastering the how-tos of decision making.

Sometime in early childhood most of us learned a vital life principle: Stop, Look, and Listen before you cross the street. Even at

that young age we were absorbing the basics of making healthy choices. Then after we grew up a little and were learning to drive, another step was added—a step that makes all the difference between a safe driver and a careless one. We were instructed to Stop, Look, Listen, *and Look Again* before we drove through an intersection or made a turn. That added component of thinking twice before we made our move helped us become better drivers. Smart Girls have added this essential element of defensive driving to their toolbox of practical life skills. When it comes to making choices, even when the road ahead seems at first glance to be clear, they take the precaution to think twice before proceeding.

> Second thoughts are ever wiser.
>
> —EURIPIDES

If you want to be a Smart Girl who lives in the power of God's *châkam*, why not look more closely at this simple process and consider, with your heart open to God's input, how you can put it into practice.

Stop—and Examine the Situation

A Smart Girl recognizes when her emotions are screaming louder than her good sense, making her susceptible to impulsive responses. She knows how to put on the brakes and stop before she goes down a road she later will wish she hadn't taken. While she tries to understand why her feelings are pulling her away from what she knows to be right, she stops herself before she gets into the quagmire of regret.

Have you ever felt a "check" in your spirit? Maybe you sensed that you needed to go another way or make another choice or say something different? That check means "Stop. Don't go any farther without considering what you're about to do." Failing to stop could send you careening into trouble.

In my life, I have noticed that sometimes these checks are just my own hesitancy, but many times they signal a definitive stop. One of the most recent checks came when I was in a conversation and began to repeat a story I'd heard. As I opened my mouth, I felt a check, and I knew it was a clear "stop," so I did.

Scientists have found that there is a "lag time"' between when we get the urge to take an action and when we actually take it. Dr. Benjamin Libet conducted studies on patients who were alert during brain surgery. By monitoring their brain activity when he asked them to move a finger, he could tell that there was a quarter-second "lag" between the urge to move the finger and the actual movement. "One-quarter of a second may not sound like much time, but in the arena of thought, it's a virtual eternity." [3] That lag gives us time to think twice about our thoughts and our perceptions, to stop and think about the situation before we make any significant move. This isn't a long pause. It's that quarter-second moment in which we stop long enough to breathe deeply and to look a bit closer at the situation.

Look—and Concentrate on Identifying the Underlying Issues

By taking a moment to stop and clear her thinking, the Smart Girl gives herself an opportunity to observe what's going on within herself, or with the other person. Going back to that story I was about to tell my friends, I can tell you that there was nothing wrong with the story. It was true, and it even had a good spiritual point. What dawned on me, however, was that one of the people in that circle of friends would have been hurt by the story I was about to share. It wasn't about her, but it would have touched on a sensitive issue in her life. As I looked at the situation, I was grateful that I'd stopped before I inadvertently caused pain to a dear friend.

Training ourselves to be aware of the underlying issues in a given situation isn't easy, especially in the middle of a hectic day or a heated encounter, but Smart Girls stop and take a deep breath before they jump in. They look and consider the whole picture instead of their own narrow view. And they listen for signals of how to respond.

Listen—Keep Your Ears Open for Helpful Insights

The original Hebrew for "tune your ears to wisdom" in Proverbs 2:2 suggests an animal's ears pricking up to hear something faint on the wind. Smart Girls are listeners. They listen more than they talk. They lean in to hear what is being said by those who are wise. They listen to the wisdom that comes from those who speak the Word of God. They even listen to the foolish with an ear toward learning what *not* to do. Smart Girls keep their ears open to learn wherever they can.

Since God is the source of all wisdom, it only makes sense to ask Him for insight and understanding. He will give it. I have found that sometimes I really haven't wanted God's wisdom because I already knew it wouldn't lean toward the choice I wanted to make. Can you identify with me? I hope so because I surely don't want to be the only one who hasn't asked because she didn't want to know! Of course, each time I've gone that route I have faced some ugly consequences, so I've grown a little smarter and don't do it as much anymore.

Look Again—and Recognize the Safety in Thinking Twice

As Proverbs 2:11 says, "Wise choices will watch over you. Understanding will keep you safe." As you seek out God-given common sense that allows you to see things for what they are, you will be given *châkam* and you will be equipped to make choices that reap positive consequences. When you take the second look in light of the wisdom that God gives, the responsibility falls on your shoulders to believe what He is saying.

A Smart Girl knows that sometimes God's wisdom leads in a direction totally opposite of what she wants to do. For example, when instinct tells her to lash back at a critic, she thinks twice and remembers that God says, "A gentle answer deflects anger, but harsh words make tempers flare" (Prov. 15:1). Trusting God enough to go against your natural response is not easy, but it's always right—and sometimes it even shocks the other person enough to bring about the desired result.

I have been the recipient of one of these unexpected, unnatural reactions, and I know how quickly it changed my attitude. I was driving through a parking lot on a bright sunny day when a young man cut right in front of me. Instead of going on my way, I gave in to an impulse of anger and followed him to his parking space. When I pulled close to him, ready to let this young man know how dangerous his driving had been, he called out, "Ma'am, I am so sorry. I was blinded by the sun. I am so sorry." Well, his words deflated my attitude like a pinhole in a balloon. He had done the opposite of what I had expected, and I was thrown totally off guard. All I could say was "That's okay. Have a good day!"

> We would be wise to be attentive and responsive to God along the way, even in matters that appear to have little significance.[4]
>
> —JERRY SITTSER

God gives us the insight we need, but we have to take it and run with it. That's what makes *châkam* work. James 1:5–6 says, "If any of you lacks wisdom, he should ask God, who gives generously to all without finding fault, and it will be given to him. But when he asks, he must believe and not doubt, because he who doubts is like a wave of the sea, blown and tossed by the wind" (NIV).

Your safeguard will be from the Lord as you trust Him to be your Protector. This is His promise when you call to Him and respect His rulership in your life.

On Your Way, Smart Girl!

If you long for the security of knowing you are thinking straight and looking at situations with a sound perspective, then embracing the principle of Stop, Look, Listen, and Look Again will propel you on your journey, and this book will provide a road map.

Becoming a Smart Girl is all about accessing and acting on the wisdom that God reserves for those who desire it and seek it in every circumstance. This is where we learn to do life with great skill. We not only do what needs to be done, but we recognize the grace we need to do it well.

We live in perilous times, and Smart Girls know that they have to consider carefully how even the most basic choices can affect their ability to enjoy a vibrant, worthwhile life that reflects God's best for them. As we'll see in the chapters ahead, your ability and willingness to think twice before you choose is essential if you're going to be an effective tool in the hands of the One who created you for His purposes.

May you and I trust God to make us intelligent, wise, caring, insightful women. May we live in the joy of *châkam*.

Chapter 1

Making Choices with Confidence

Smart Girls Think Twice About Consequences

My mother and daddy met in a class at business college. He had a limited education but thick, dark hair and loads of wit and charm. She was a blonde-haired, blue-eyed beauty who doggedly put herself through college despite suffering the loss of her mother at the age of eighteen. Both were trying to better their chances for employment by taking the business course, but the biggest bonus to come out of that class was their meeting one another.

Each day they shared a package of crackers and a Coca-Cola for lunch. This bonded them together on a life journey that would last more than fifty-five years. Daddy often told me that when Mother walked into the classroom, he said to himself, "I'm going to marry that woman"—and marry her he did. I, their only child, was born five years later. The effects of the choices they made way back then continue to this very day.

That's the way of choices: they always have consequences, many of which last longer than we initially could imagine. The word *consequences* sounds as if it always involves punishment, but it doesn't. Consequences are simply the inevitable results of a choice, whether positive or negative. Every choice we make will bring consequences of some kind.

I learned about this relationship between choice and consequence at an early age by watching as my parents made big choices with great hopes and often huge consequences. In their early years, they lived hand to mouth. Mother stayed home to care for me and to make a home out of our tiny house. Daddy worked at a filling station owned by Mr. B. O. Jennings. (I love that name.) He pumped gas, washed car windows, changed oil and tires, and kept track of the money, a small percentage of which comprised his salary. It soon became clear that the money my dad brought in just wasn't enough for our family. My parents loved each other, and they loved me, but they did not love the financial future they saw stretching before them. So they thought about making a life change, and then they thought again. They came to the conclusion that moving where there were good jobs was the best choice for them. Daddy quit his job in Birmingham, Alabama, and got on a bus headed north.

He arrived in Washington DC on a cold January day. For more than two weeks he walked the streets answering ads and looking anywhere he could for work, but no job offers were made. Though lonely and discouraged, he had no intention of giving up. He had thought once, he had thought twice, and the choice had been made. His settled conviction gave him a certain confidence. So he called and asked my mother to catch the bus to Washington and come be with him. She did just that, and with my little two-year-old self in tow, she arrived at the Greyhound bus station after an all-night ride to find Daddy waiting with open arms to take us to the rented room where we would make our new home together.

He had found a one-room flat with a double bed and two over-stuffed chairs that could be pushed together to make a wonderful crib. There was no refrigerator, but a handsome windowsill would keep my milk cold. There was no stove, but we had a hot plate to warm soup and a great little mom-and-pop restaurant waited just around the corner. What more could we need? Oh yes, there was a bathroom—down the hall!

My parents had considered their situation and made a life-changing choice, and we lived with the consequences of that choice from then on.

As a consequence of my parents' choice, not only did we live for a time in a one-room flat but I got to grow up near the nation's capital, surrounded by museums, art galleries, libraries, streetcars, and buses. I could go and see just about anything my curious mind wanted to take in.

As a consequence of my parents' choice, my dad ultimately found a good job and was able to provide a modest but stable income for our family for his entire working life.

> There are two primary choices in our lives: to accept conditions as they exist or accept the responsibility for changing them.[1]
>
> —DENIS WAITLEY

As a consequence of my parents' choice, my mother met a school principal who invited her to teach in an elementary school. For more than twenty years, my mother taught fifth grade in an excellent school system.

As a consequence of my parents' choice, I was able to gain a college education without struggling to pay for it.

As a consequence of my parents' choice, I was brought up in a solid, loving church where I heard the Word of God on a regular basis. (It took a while for the consequences of that choice to be revealed, but it was an outcome of their choice, nonetheless.)

As I watched, listened, and experienced my parents' journey, I became intimately acquainted with the reality that choices must be made. I learned that it is impossible to go through life without deciding between the possibilities that wait behind Doors One, Two, and Three. Trying to play it safe by only *looking* at the Doors of Opportunity and declining to fling one open simply sets in motion a different set of consequences. We cannot avoid making choices; it's an integral part of being human that goes back to the very beginning of time. God purposefully left choice in our hands. He could have made us little automatons, but instead He chose to give us free will, leaving us with the responsibility and the pleasure of making our own decisions.

The First Taste of Consequences

Eve, of Adam and Eve fame, was the first girl in all of history to make a choice—and the first to face the consequences of that choice. Let's take a quick look at the drama that played out in the garden of Eden so long ago.

> The serpent was clever, more clever than any wild animal GOD had made. He spoke to the Woman: "Do I understand that God told you not to eat from any tree in the garden?"
>
> The Woman said to the serpent, "Not at all. We can eat from the trees in the garden. It's only about the tree in the middle of the garden that God said, 'Don't eat from it; don't even touch it or you'll die.'" (Gen. 3:1–3 MSG)

Sounds to me like God had given Adam and Eve a simple, easy-to-follow command with clear and established consequences for disobedience. Unfortunately, Eve moved on impulse rather than thinking twice.

> The serpent told the Woman, "You won't die. God knows that the moment you eat from that tree, you'll see what's really going on. You'll be just like God, knowing everything, ranging all the way from good to evil."
> When the Woman saw that the tree looked like good eating and realized what she would get out of it—she'd know everything!—she took and ate the fruit and then gave some to her husband, and he ate. (Gen. 3:4–6 MSG)

Eve chose poorly and soon discovered she would pay a high price in negative consequences.

> GOD said, . . . "Did you eat from that tree I told you not to eat from?"
> The Man said, "The Woman you gave me as a companion, she gave me fruit from the tree, and, yes, I ate it."
> GOD said to the Woman, "What is this that you've done?"
> "The serpent seduced me," she said, "and I ate." (Gen. 3:11–13 MSG)

Ah, the blame game. Eve had failed in making the most important choice of her life, and Adam had joined in her folly. Each offered excuses and pointed at someone else to bear the blame for the fiasco, but that did not change the consequences: death had come—death to all they had, all they had dreamed of, and all they had relied on. It seemed they had assumed God would always keep them in the manner to which they had become accustomed, but He did not alter the appointed consequences for their blatant disobedience just because they were tempted by the enemy. They still bore the responsibility for their choice.

He told the Woman:

"I'll multiply your pains in childbirth;

you'll give birth to your babies in pain.

You'll want to please your husband,

but he'll lord it over you."

He told the Man:

"Because you listened to your wife

and ate from the tree

That I commanded you not to eat from,

'Don't eat from this tree,'

The very ground is cursed because of you;

getting food from the ground

Will be as painful as having babies is for your wife;

you'll be working in pain all your life long." (Gen. 3:16–17 MSG)

Choices inevitably bring consequences; it was quite a lesson for the first girl in history to learn. Sometimes it's easy to look at others, particularly our grandmother Eve, and think that, given the opportunity, we would not have fallen for the manipulations of the enemy. And yet when it comes to our own choices, we find that thinking twice and being smart is not as easy as it may seem. Like Eve, we find ourselves tempted to respond on impulse and rush headlong into a devastating decision. "For the world offers only a craving for physical pleasure, a craving for everything we see, and pride in our achievements and possessions" (1 John 2:16).

Our cravings and our pride make good choices difficult, especially if we haven't decided ahead of time what principles will guide our decision-making process. It's hard to choose against eating that luscious piece of cake even though we know it will undermine our attempts to slim down. It's hard to put that darling outfit back on the store hanger when it fits perfectly but is out of our price range. And it's hard to say no to a great job offer that strokes the ego even when we know it would take us away during a time when our kids and husbands need us. That's why the second thought, that deeper consideration of potential consequences, is so crucial to making the best choices possible. As the master seamstress reminds her student, "Measure twice, cut once!" Choice without regret is a wonderful thing.

Compound Interest and Poor Choices

When it comes to choices, we have to be aware of the principle of compound interest. As with a successful investment, each positive choice you make increases your capital as a Smart Girl and puts you in a better position to make future choices. By contrast, every poor choice, like an ever-growing debt, accrues interest that must be paid.

Shannon knows this better than most. As an idealistic fifteen-year-old, she thought she knew everything. She knew she loved Jim, who was twenty, but she also knew her parents wouldn't let her get married. She believed that if she slept with him, he would stay around until she was old enough to marry. She didn't factor in the possibility of contracting a sexually transmitted disease. Eventually a strange pain down one leg and flu-like symptoms prompted a visit to her doctor. When he said, "You have herpes simplex virus," her teenage mind couldn't understand what

> Every choice carries a consequence. For better or worse, each choice is the unavoidable consequence of its predecessor.[2]
>
> —GARY RYAN BLAIR

that meant. So the doctor told her the painful truth about how she'd become infected and the lack of a cure. She knew something was terribly wrong, but she had no idea then how it would affect her life. She stopped seeing Jim, disgusted with herself and disgusted with him. He tucked tail and willingly ran, but she was left with the consequences.

Now at age thirty Shannon knows all too well the effects of her choice because she's still paying compound interest on the consequences of sleeping with Jim. She's had several herpes outbreaks over the years since her diagnosis although they have become less severe. She grew up, went off to college, and became a successful marketing executive with a large firm.

Then a year or so ago she met the love of her life at church. Eric is handsome and godly. He treats her like a queen, and she adores him. They're talking about marriage, but she knows that before she can say yes, she will have to face up to telling him about her past choice and the resulting consequences. She'll have to say, "I'd love to marry you, but you need to know that I have a sexually transmitted disease that can affect you." It feels overwhelming, and Shannon is torn about what to do. What will Eric think? Is he going to want to have "protected" sex for the rest of their married lives? Will he want her to carry his children? Should she tell him that any children born to her will need to be specially protected during birth to prevent them from contracting her disease? Since she hasn't had an outbreak in a couple of years, is it safe not to tell him and just hope for the best? What would she do if he found out? What would she do if she infected him?

Oh, the mortification of a bad choice and, oh, the ongoing effects of compound interest. As negative consequences pile up, it can quickly feel as if you'll always be trapped in debt to the past. The simple answer seems complex, the hard decision seems impossible, and the temptation to pile on more poor choices becomes almost overwhelming. The only way to resist is to deliberately choose to think twice and carefully weigh the consequences.

To break the cycle before she makes another poor choice, Shannon needs to Stop and examine the situation, Look to identify the issues, Listen for insight from the Lord, and then Look Again as she waits for the Lord to give her *châkam*. With the choice she makes, either she will prove herself a Smart Girl with an intelligent attitude toward life or she will revert to the old, immature thinking that brought about the consequence with its compound interest in the first place.

What Consequences Might You Be Overlooking?

I recently had dinner with a group of women who could hold master's degrees from the School of Bad Choices and Miserable Consequences. In the setting of a church fellowship hall, they looked just like any group of friends enjoying a girls' night out. They bantered, laughed, and talked about clothes, children, and men as girlfriends often do. But these seemingly lighthearted women were newly released from our local corrections facility, otherwise known as a prison.

At one point I asked a question that sobered the conversation: "Knowing what you know now, what would you think twice about next time? What choices would you make differently?"

A hand shot up at the back of the room. "I'd think twice about wanting to experience drugs. I just had to try them, and I ended up on the streets. I became a prostitute. They are so strong, so powerful. Even tonight I want to get high."

Another hand went up. "I thought I had to be independent so early. I chose to leave home, to be on my own."

And another hand. "I chose sex at an early age. I never thought of the consequences. It was just what I wanted to do!"

The next woman acknowledged, "I never thought the things I was doing would have an effect on my children. Now I know I hurt them with my choices. But I never gave it a second thought until I went to prison and I saw their pain."

The hands just kept coming. "I should have thought about who I was hanging out with."

"I thought I could handle everything myself."

"I should have thought twice about the financial commitments I made."

"I should have thought about how to deal with temptation. I didn't think I could say no."

The lives of these women perfectly illustrate the maxim that "sin will take you farther than you ever intended to stray, cost you more than you ever intended to pay, and keep you longer than you ever intended to stay."[3] Each one had paid dearly for her failure to think twice by enduring the harsh consequences of her choices. But, of course, you don't have to end up in prison to experience the devastating penalties of compound interest on poor choices.

- More than fifty percent of the marriages in this country reportedly end in divorce.[4] Could thinking twice have helped some of those women avoid the pain of such a division—or led them to avoid a painful marriage to begin with?

- Countless children are vulnerable because someone hasn't thought twice about the danger of an overly interested neighbor, relative, or teacher. What devastating consequences could be headed off by someone asking, "What's going on?" or "Is this an appropriate interaction?"

- Many friendships have ended in disappointment because too much was shared too soon. A second thought before "telling all" would have spared some women the hurt of realizing that certain things should be kept private.

- The Internet has made it all too easy to strike up inappropriate relationships with the opposite sex, and women quickly find themselves snared by the tentacles of an emotional affair—and sometimes more. Consider the heartache that could be avoided by thinking twice about the potentially disastrous effects of cyberflirting.

It's never too late to turn around your thinking. But keep in mind that, like a rusty bolt, the longer you stay locked in position, the greater the effort required to slide toward healthier choices and the positive consequences they bring. The second look can give you a clearer perspective of how things are rather than how you wish they were. Even if you don't like what you see, looking again gives you an opportunity to make a good choice.

For example, when their teenagers started down a road to rebellion, many a parent has been grateful that they had the common sense to see it for what it was rather than choosing to look the other way and hope the behavior would go away.

Taking that second look every time, whether you think you need to or not, is a healthy way to get your thinking going in the right direction. Consider that initial guilt you sometimes feel when you decline to sign up for a volunteer project because your heart isn't in it. Thinking twice about the situation might give you the insight to remember the truth that "it is God who is at work in you, both to will and to work for His good pleasure" (Phil. 2:13 NASB). God gave you your desires and abilities, so anytime you feel a gnawing doubt about a situation, give it that second look. God may be speaking to you about a better choice for your time and attention.

Tune In to the Lessons All Around You

The process of shifting our perspective and thinking twice about consequences is not accomplished in a vacuum. One of the ways we "tune [our] ears to wisdom, and concentrate on understanding" (Prov. 2:2) is by being alert to what's happening with the people around us. Smart Girls intentionally seek out people who clearly are making good choices. The Scripture says, "Become wise by walking with the wise; hang out with fools and watch your life fall to pieces" (Prov. 13:20 MSG). That advice is about as plain as it gets.

One of the basic principles for making good choices is prick up your ears and listen. We all can learn from one another.

Look around at the people in your world. If their lives are working because they have made good choices, lean into their space and figure out how they do it. If they're content with their lives, find out why. If they have a thankful heart for whatever they have, pay attention to how their words and actions nurture gratitude. If they have well-behaved children, watch how they handle them. If they have a healthy marriage, watch how they treat their mates. If they express a sincere confidence in God even in the midst of difficulty, listen for clues about how they have learned to trust Him. If they excel at their work yet keep life in balance, notice how they manage their time. Watch! And then after you have watched, emulate what they do.

We also can learn from those who are suffering because of poor choices. The grace of God is often most tangible around these people. None of us makes smart choices all the time, so there are bound to be people in your life this very minute who are struggling and yet at the same time listening for wisdom, eager to hear what the Lord is saying to them. This is a great time to draw near with an open heart. You can listen and learn from their experiences even as you pray for the mercy and compassion each person needs amid consequences gone awry.

Of course, not all difficulties result from bad choices. Jesus spoke clearly on this subject when the disciples mistakenly made a broad assumption about a man born blind. As you read this revealing scene, picture yourself standing among the disciples, listening and concentrating in this teachable moment with the Master.

> As Jesus was walking along, he saw a man who had been blind from birth. "Rabbi," his disciples asked him, "why was this man born blind? Was it because of his own sins or his parents' sins?"
>
> "It was not because of his sins or his parents' sins," Jesus answered. "This happened so the power of God could be seen in him." (John 9:1–3)

Jesus' words were simple and straightforward. The man's condition was not a consequence of someone's choice; he was just blind. But there was a reason. There always is a reason for whatever challenge or opportunity we face, although we may not know it on this earth. When we face circumstances beyond our control, we are given the option to respond with wisdom or to react with folly. What we choose will determine the course of our lives.

We can learn from every experience if we will examine the situation, look at the underlying issues, listen for wisdom, and recognize the safety of thinking twice. The Smart Girl knows that every challenge offers a *châkam* moment.

Recognize the Limits of Logic

Even when we make the best choice we can with the information we have, life is full of uncertainties. We give ourselves the very best chance of succeeding when we think twice, but continually second-guessing yourself and waffling about your choice is just as debilitating as jumping in headlong with no consideration of what might happen as a result. Such agonizing can paralyze your thinking as you keep rehearsing the negatives to the point that you can't see the possibilities.

You won't enjoy the good decisions you have made if you are constantly looking over your shoulder wondering, *What if I had done it differently? Is it too late to make a change?* Because of my life experience, making choices feels like an adventure to me. I don't fear making them. Others, many times because of their life experiences, find themselves twisted inside out each time they face a choice. If this describes you, I understand. Anxiety over the potential consequences of your decisions can make you feel as if your life is a field riddled with land mines just waiting to explode.

Sherry struggled for much of her life with the inability to make a decision. As a teenager, she was forced to make choices that were way over her head while being constantly admonished to "think before you act." Her parents threw her into the deep waters of responsibility with little advice but plenty of harsh and noninstructive words. As a sixteen-year-old, she was told that if she wanted a car, she'd have to earn the money to buy it herself, which she did. Her father refused to go with her to choose a car, but when she came home with her purchase, he promptly upbraided her. "Why did you buy that car? Don't you know it doesn't get good mileage? It's just a piece of junk. What were you thinking?"

> If you choose not to decide, you still have made a choice.
>
> —FROM "FREEWILL," LYRICS BY NEIL PEART

Of course, Sherry wilted under his disparagement and immediately tried to take the car back. She tried every way she could to finagle the previous owner into giving her money back, but he wouldn't budge; a deal was a deal. So she drove home in her long-anticipated first car with tears running down her face. "How could I be so stupid? Why didn't I check on the gas mileage? How am I going to be able to afford this car?"

She lived at home a few more years, during which her dad seemed always ready to point out where she had missed the mark. Then she went away to college. She paid as many bills as she could from her job as a checkout clerk at the grocery store, and she covered the rest with student loans. Every choice made Sherry nervous. Was she doing the right thing? Was she taking the right classes? Was she dating the right guy? Would her dad approve? Was she really the loser he seemed to think she was? Self-doubt permeated her every decision, so she often put off choosing until the last minute and then frequently tried to change or cancel her choice.

Only after marrying a great guy, who patiently led her to understand that few choices are either absolutely perfect or completely flawed, has Sherry been able to do better in her choice making. She still hesitates, still second-guesses herself, but she is learning to do the best she can with what she knows and then trust God with the consequences. She's discovered that He is easy to consult and faithful to answer. Even though from time to time her old insecurities creep in, she *makes* herself decide and then diligently reasons with herself about the truth she now knows: unlike her father, who didn't know how to love his daughter, her heavenly Father is always there and more than willing to help her out when she needs it.

Like Sherry, you and I need to know that we will sometimes face choices for which the consequences cannot be fully predicted. Often this happens when we're called upon to do something we know is right but we feel uncertain about where that choice will lead. A great question to ask at these moments is "When is it right to do right?" Of course, the answer is "always."

When we face such choices, we have to guard against letting fear dominate our thinking. The unknown is a scary place, but we all have to go there when we are called upon to make good decisions without guarantees. That is one of the reasons we see the phrase "be strong and courageous" so often in Scripture (Deut. 31:6–7; Josh. 1:6–7, 9; 10:25; 1 Chron. 22:13; Ps. 31:24). Knowing God and believing that "where He guides, He provides"[5] is the key to strength and courage. Even though we cannot always see the consequences that await us, we have a God who not only lives in our present but also dwells in our future. If you know God, really know Him on a personal basis, you can do what you know is right, confident that He has your back, your front, and both sides covered. The consequences are in His hands, and you are safe with Him. Your task is to choose the path you know is right, refuse to look back in worry, and remind yourself to be like the psalmist who said, "My eyes are always on the LORD" (Ps. 25:15).

The story of Jochebed, mother of Moses, presents a powerful example of a woman making the best choice she can under seemingly impossible circumstances and with no guarantee of the results. Let's take a look at her situation:

> Then Pharaoh gave this order to all his people: "Every boy that is born you must throw into the Nile, but let every girl live."
>
> Now a man of the house of Levi married a Levite woman, and she became pregnant and gave birth to a son. (Exod. 1:22–2:2 NIV)

Try to put yourself in this woman's sandals. What would you do, given her two options? Either you could throw your baby in the Nile to face certain death, or you could do what little you could to save your child and leave the rest of the story with God. Let's see what Jochebed chose.

> When she saw that he was a fine child, she hid him for three months. But when she could hide him no longer, she got a papyrus basket for him and coated it with tar and pitch. Then she placed the child in it and put it among the reeds along the bank of the Nile. His sister stood at a distance to see what would happen to him.
>
> Then Pharaoh's daughter went down to the Nile to bathe, and her attendants were walking along the river bank. She saw the basket among the reeds and sent her slave girl to get it. She

opened it and saw the baby. He was crying, and she felt sorry for him. "This is one of the Hebrew babies," she said.

Then his sister asked Pharaoh's daughter, "Shall I go and get one of the Hebrew women to nurse the baby for you?"

"Yes, go," she answered. And the girl went and got the baby's mother. Pharaoh's daughter said to her, "Take this baby and nurse him for me, and I will pay you." So the woman took the baby and nursed him. When the child grew older, she took him to Pharaoh's daughter and he became her son. She named him Moses, saying, "I drew him out of the water." (Exod. 2:2–10 NIV)

This story always touches a tender place in my heart. I have nothing but respect for this woman of great courage. Like any of us, she would have preferred to raise her own son to adulthood, but she was forced to make a choice without guarantees. She had no idea of the consequences, but she knew putting her baby in the Nile to drown was not a choice she could make. So she did what she could by making him that little waterproof basket, and then she did what she had to by releasing him into the Nile and into God's hands. Jochebed gets my vote for being a superior Smart Girl.

And her story provides a lesson for all of us who face tough choices about our children. I call it "Moses's Mama's Principle" and it goes like this: do what you can and leave the rest to God.

This principle came into play for Kristen, a single mother of three young boys and one teenager bent on testing every limit he could. She knew that she could not allow the behavior of her older son, Marcus, to continue influencing his young brothers, and she also knew that her ex-husband was willing to have their son live with him. She worried that sending Marcus away would damage their relationship even further, but the current situation clearly wasn't working. Then one weekend he broke the house rules yet again and the whole scene exploded. He came in at 2:00 a.m., disrespected his mother with back talk, then picked on his brothers unmercifully when he finally got out of bed the next day. Kristen thought twice about the choice she had to make with no guarantees of a positive outcome. Then with fear and trembling, she told Marcus he had to leave. Of course, his departure was marked by all the drama he could create. After vowing never to come back in the house and never to speak to her again, he slammed the door on his way out.

> The lot is cast into the lap, but its every decision is from the LORD.
>
> —PROVERBS 16:33 NASB

True to his word, over the next two years Marcus remained withdrawn and sullen, avoiding all of his mother's attempts to make contact. She sent him notes and tried to see him in the school parking lot. He would have none of it and tried to punish her as much as he could. This child she loved with all of her heart seemed determined to test every ounce of faith and trust that she had placed in God. She clung to the words of Romans 8:28: "And we know that God causes everything to work together for the good of those who love God and are called according to his purpose for them." She knew that when the Bible uses the word *everything*, it truly means *everything*, including the rebellious, headstrong behavior of a teenage son. Kristen also knew that the core issue for her was not loving her son and making a hard choice concerning him; rather, her challenge was to love God and believe that He was in control of the future. She had no guarantees that the consequence of her hard decision would be good. She just knew that she had considered the best choice to make, she had called out to God, she had thought twice, and then she had gone ahead.

And her decision was affirmed at last. After finding his own relationship with Christ, Marcus came back home at the age of eighteen with a totally changed attitude.

Of course, not all of our choices will turn out as we hope. That's life. Sometimes, even though we think twice, there simply is no perfect choice; other times the right choice is obvious but just plain difficult. The best we can do is Stop, Look, Listen, and Look Again at the possible consequences of each option—then make the wisest choice we can, leaving the rest in God's capable hands. There is great relief in knowing that God sees and God cares and, ultimately, God is in control.

Chapter 2

For Real—It's a Warning!

Smart Girls Think Twice About Red Flags

t looked as if it had been dropped on my kitchen floor and left there just to give me the creeps—and it worked! I gingerly picked it up, inspected it a little closer to make sure I wasn't imagining things, and then quickly threw it away. I tried to dismiss it from my mind. I told myself I didn't need to take it seriously.

When my husband came downstairs, I asked his opinion. He, too, dismissed it as insignificant, suggesting that he'd probably tracked it into the house on his boot after having been in the woods that day. In light of this totally reasonable explanation, I relaxed and determined not to worry about it. Finding a four-inch piece of snake skin on the kitchen floor surely did not mean a snake was lurking close by.

I completely failed to recognize that snake skin as a red flag—

a warning signal alerting me to a potential hazard. As clear as that sign may seem now, at the time I ignored it, cruising along in denial and finding comfort in a common-sense explanation. I wasn't looking for snakes, I didn't want to see a snake, and as far as I was concerned, there was no reasonable way a snake could have left that skin on my kitchen floor, never mind that we lived in the middle of two acres of woods. So I went on, business as usual.

The next red flag was bigger and demanded more attention. Our son Aaron called my cell phone from our house, where he'd gone to pick up his dog, whom we babysat frequently. He said that as he was preparing to leave, his dog spotted a snake curled up under a stool and threw it in the air. The snake had crawled under the refrigerator and now he couldn't reach it. We were only two minutes away, so we quickly arrived in our driveway. Aaron's wife was sitting in their car, holding their dog.

As we got out of the car, I shouted to her, "What kind of snake was it?"

She said, "It was little and green."

I immediately reverted to my happy state of denial. Little and green? No big deal.

The guys got busy tilting the refrigerator back and forth, trying to get at the snake. I took the opportunity to reach underneath to clear out the dust bunnies. Remember, I believed the scaly intruder was little and green. (Later, I found out my son had downplayed his description of the snake to his wife because he didn't want to upset her! Upset *her*?)

Failing to find the snake, Aaron left, and Charlie went up to bed. I got a glass of water from the refrigerator dispenser, then sat down to leaf through the newspaper and process our adventure before I went to bed. Little did I know there was more processing to come.

As I was looking down at the paper, something just at the edge of my vision caught my attention. I looked up to find not a four-inch piece of skin but at least fourteen inches of a mottled brown, writhing snake. A quilt-size red flag this time. The alert finally registered.

I shouted to Charlie, "It is not little, and it is not green! I need help!"

Between us, we were able to pin down the snake and kill him. After that animated struggle, we both sighed with relief. Then as we bagged the snake to put it in the garbage can, we checked it more closely and recognized it as a copperhead, a poisonous snake common to our area. We were even more grateful. A real live snake had been in our house, but no one had been bitten and the snake was gone. End of story. Or so we thought.

> A danger foreseen is half avoided.
>
> —ANONYMOUS

Then came two more sightings that traced the snake's little tour of our home. Another part of his skin was found in a closet and, horror of horrors, the carpet cleaners found the rest of his skin behind a large piece of furniture in the living room.

Reality finally dawned on me: I need help with this. A deadly snake has been crawling all over the downstairs of my house, and I didn't know it. Does he have family that lives here too? Are his cousins planning to move in and, if so, where's their secret entrance?

I checked the yellow pages and called the snake eradicator. He came immediately and did what snake eradicators do. He plugged up tiny holes around the foundation on the outside and scattered pellets around the yard to burn the belly of any snake that dared to approach in the future.

My snake problem has now been conquered, but I never will forget that by ignoring the first red flag, we allowed something dangerous and dark to stay in our home way too long. That's the thing about red flags. They are there for a reason: to signal you to stop and pay attention because danger lies ahead.

Caution: Danger Ahead

Smart Girls know how to recognize red flags in every area of life from relationships to finances, from parenting to physical dangers.

Have you ever had a bad feeling about a relationship that just didn't seem quite right?

Did you ever feel a twinge of discomfort about the unworthy content of a movie you were watching or a book you were reading?

Have you ever felt less than satisfied with an explanation of your teen's whereabouts?

Has a friend ever warned you about doing business with a particular company?

Has your doctor urged you to quit smoking or lose weight?

Red flags are all around, warning us to Stop, Look, Listen, and Look Again before proceeding. Yet how often do we pick and choose which ones we will heed? Have you, like me, dealt with some uncomfortable consequences because you rushed past a red flag? Or maybe you've seen the red flag and kept right on going, believing that since nothing bad has happened so far there's no reason to worry.

Many of us fall victim to the familiar "dodging the bullet" syndrome. We have emerged relatively unscathed from risky behaviors and assume that we always will be immune to the consequences. The truth remains that red flags are there for a reason, even when we can't yet see that reason.

Ask the sun worshiper who ignored for years the warnings about the dangers of ultraviolet radiation. Now she's dealing with skin cancer and facing an uncertain prognosis.

Ask the woman who married the man her friends tried to tell

her was bad news. Now she's trying to find a way to escape her abusive husband.

Ask the person who cosigned a car loan for a friend having credit trouble. Now that friend's credit trouble has become hers.

Ask the lonely woman who thought she could trust her neighbor with her deepest secret, despite how freely that neighbor shared others' secrets with her. Now she's embarrassed to go grocery shopping because her private life has been spread all over her small town.

Ask the parents who saw their daughter playing with the food on her plate and losing weight at an alarming rate but did nothing about it. Now they're in an anorexia rehab unit, watching their once-beautiful little girl fight for her life.

To ignore red flags and foolishly declare, "Oh, that will never happen" is to put yourself and possibly those you love in danger. But Smart Girls know that red flags serve a valuable purpose. They are not there to keep you from having a good time or from moving forward with what you want to do; red flags serve as reminders to think carefully before you proceed. Sometimes the flags signal a detour that leads to the same destination; sometimes they advise you to stop and wait for a better time; and sometimes they caution you that moving ahead will put you in certain peril. In every case, when you're willing to heed them and to think twice about what they reveal, red flags can protect you from unnecessary pain and frustration.

Ten Red Flags You Can't Afford to Ignore

While warning signals come in all shapes and sizes and areas of life, God gave ten unmistakable red flags to the children of Israel and all the generations following, which includes us. In Exodus 20:3–17 we find the Lord's instructions to His people, warnings against behaviors and attitudes that lead to certain disaster. Choosing to ignore

God's kindness to us in posting these red-flag commandments can be the undoing of who we are as individuals and as a nation. By contrast, when we observe His warnings we find ourselves traveling a road along which His grace and our lives can flourish.

So let's look at each of these red flags and what they mean for Smart Girls.

1. Accept No Substitutes

God knows that when we begin to seek answers for our lives there always will be some substitute god enticing us away from Him with the promise of peace and prosperity. That's why He warns, "You must not have any other god but me" (Exod. 20:3). He desires to have a monogamous relationship with us. It breaks His heart when we look to other sources to fulfill His role in our lives. It brings Him to anger when we choose to worship other people, other philosophies, or other providers when He is the One who started our hearts beating in our mothers' wombs before they even knew we were there.

Satan—God's archenemy and ours—is masterful at presenting alternative gods wrapped in wonder and light. Little *g* gods don't always have a persona or a physical shape; they can be found behind simple concepts such as *drawing power from cosmic energy* or *worshiping the universe.*

Recently, the ancient idea of the *universal law of attraction* has reemerged in *The Secret* by Rhonda Byrne and garnered a huge following of people desperate for hope. This so-called law essentially elevates man to be the master of his own fate. Its proponents assert that the secret to getting everything you ever have wanted is ask, believe, and you will receive because in so doing, you attract good things to yourself.

How Satan loves to counterfeit God's blessings by giving a perverted little twist in his presentation. When he questioned why

God had instructed Adam and Eve not to eat from the tree in the middle of the garden, his words subtly conveyed the message, "God's holding out on you, and God doesn't mean what He says. You don't need Him; you can take what you want for yourself." As we saw in chapter 1, our dear grandmother Eve fell for the lie, and here we are.

Calling God's goodness a *gift from the universe* negates the fact that He has a name, and He is the Creator of the universe. If we just talk about an impersonal universe, then we don't have to deal with a personal God who has the right to be involved in our lives because He created not only the universe but us as well. If He is your God, then you are a person of His "very own possession" (1 Pet. 2:9). His care, protection, and provision are yours. You don't have to attract good things to yourself. He will give you what you need, when you need it, and you will enjoy the spiritual and mental contentment of knowing that meaning in your life comes not from what you can do but from what He does in you, through you, and to you.

Of course the enemy uses many other tools of deception to entice us away from truth. Years ago I became involved in the study of reincarnation, another one of those philosophies that cuts God out of the equation. I hate to think where I would be today if I had continued toying with the belief that we never have to die because there are many lives to live. But then I encountered the Scripture that says, "Each person is destined to die once and after that comes judgment" (Heb. 9:27). That verse brought truth to my deluded soul and set me back on the right course.

Have you, too, gone after other gods, maybe bought into one of the do-it-yourself philosophies? If so, this girl understands. The good news is that the God who is jealous for our affection and allegiance also is merciful and forgiving of our folly. When we chase after other gods, it breaks His heart because He loves us so deeply, and He always waits with open arms to take us back.

2. Be Careful To Whom and What You Cozy Up

Hand in hand with the preceding instruction comes this warning: "You must not make for yourself an idol of any kind . . . for I, the LORD your God, am a jealous God who will not tolerate your affection for any other gods" (Exod. 20:4–5). Smart Girls take these words to heart and think twice about anything that vies for their affection.

This red flag carries particular significance these days as we constantly encounter new ideas and trends in our multicultural society. I know that decorating with Buddhas and lotus flowers is popular now, but it troubles me to see believers accepting a big, old smiling Buddha as a natural part of their décor. The last thing on earth I want to be is legalistic. My heart and mind have been changed by the sweet grace of God and that is what I want to offer to others, but I wonder how God must feel when we cavalierly accept another god, created by human hands, as an integral part of our decorating scheme?

Romans 1 gives us further insight into this matter of allowing idols into our lives:

> They know the truth about God because he has made it obvious to them. For ever since the world was created, people have seen the earth and sky. Through everything God made, they can clearly see his invisible qualities—his eternal power and divine nature. So they have no excuse for not knowing God. (vv. 19–20)

No excuse. God has clearly revealed Himself and His nature to us. Yet watch what happens next.

> Yes, they knew God, but they wouldn't worship him as God or even give him thanks. And they began to think up foolish ideas of what God was like. As a result, their minds became dark and

confused. Claiming to be wise, they instead became utter fools. And instead of worshiping the glorious, ever-living God, they worshiped idols made to look like mere people and birds and animals and reptiles.

So God abandoned them to do whatever shameful things their hearts desired. As a result, they did vile and degrading things with each other's bodies. They traded the truth about God for a lie. So they worshiped and served the things God created instead of the Creator himself, who is worthy of eternal praise! (vv. 21–25)

Take a look around. You and I are surrounded by things God has created. Whether you take pleasure in the natural world or the material world, God is the One behind it all. Children are a gift from God, but they are not God. Friends and lovers are created by God, but they are not God. Houses and land spring forth from the creativity of God, but they are not God. All the wonderful things that bring joy to our lives are blessings from God, but they are not God.

It's easy to become so enamored with the things God has given for our pleasure and delight that we miss Him. How hurtful it must be to God when we wrap our hands around the gifts He has given and cling to them as if our whole lives depended on them! When we worship what we have and forget who gave it to us, we fall into a trap that can only cause us pain.

God is the giver. He is the one from whose hand we receive every good thing. He is also the taker. He is the one who can take it all away. Job, a man whom God held up to the challenge of Satan as a perfect man, said,

> I was naked when I was born,
> and I will be naked when I die.

> The LORD gave these things to me,
> and he has taken them away.
> Praise the name of the LORD. (Job 1:21 NCV)

God knows our hearts, and He wants to give us good things to satisfy our longings, but more than anything He wants to be the one in whom our souls find ultimate satisfaction. When this is true we can honestly say, "I don't want to live without _____ (fill in the blank), but I can live without it because God is my strength and my redeemer. Praise the name of the Lord!"

3. One Name Is Above All Others

The Bible warns, "You must not misuse the name of the LORD your God. The LORD will not let you go unpunished if you misuse his name" (Exod. 20:7). Yet how casually we seem to throw around the name of the Lord. The phrase "Oh, my God" belongs only in prayer, but I've heard it used in response to everything from winning a prize at the state fair to hearing the devastating news that Grandpa has had a stroke.

The careless way so many of us use the name of the Lord only demonstrates that we don't understand the importance of His name. Once as I was boarding a plane, I reached up to put my package in the overhead compartment. A Jewish man seated in my row stood up and said, "Wait, wait. I have something with the name of the Lord on it. I don't want you to put your bag on top of it." I assured him that I revered the name of the Lord and understood. After that we had a great conversation. Although he was Jewish and I am Christian, we both call on the name of the same Lord, the God of Abraham, Isaac, and Jacob.

This is the same God who spoke to Moses when it was time for him to lead the sons of Israel out of captivity in Egypt and into the Promised Land. Moses had his reservations, but God spoke to him with great authority. Take a moment to read this scenario, and then see how you feel about the name of God.

> But Moses said to God, "Who am I that I should go to Pharaoh, and that I should bring the children of Israel out of Egypt? . . . Indeed, when I come to the children of Israel and say to them, 'The God of your fathers has sent me to you,' and they say to me, 'What is His name?' what shall I say to them?"
>
> And God said to Moses, "I AM WHO I AM." And He said, "Thus you shall say to the children of Israel, 'I AM has sent me to you.'" Moreover God said to Moses, "Thus you shall say to the children of Israel: 'The LORD God of your fathers, the God of Abraham, the God of Isaac, and the God of Jacob, has sent me to you. This is My name forever, and this is My memorial to all generations.'" (Exod. 3:11, 13–15 NKJV)

The name of God is holy, set apart and different from all others. When His Son came to earth in human form to redeem us from our sins, He continued to be God but His earthly name was Jesus.

Let's read the account of the angel's appearance to Mary, the mother of Jesus, telling her about this name:

> Then the angel said to her, "Do not be afraid, Mary, for you have found favor with God. And behold, you will conceive in your womb and bring forth a Son, and shall call His name JESUS. He will be great, and will be called the Son of the Highest; and the Lord God will give Him the throne of His father David. And He will reign over the house of Jacob forever, and of His kingdom there will be no end." (Luke 1:30–33 NKJV)

The names of God and Jesus are set apart in our lives. To be cavalier about how we use those names is to be careless about

God. Yet casual use has become such a habit for most people that they don't even hear what they're saying. If this is true for you, how would you feel about putting a rubber band on your wrist as a reminder to be aware of your words? When you hear yourself saying God's name outside of prayer or appropriate conversation, give yourself a little snap with the rubber band and see if that little sting helps you remember that His name is holy. If you have fallen into using the name of Jesus as a slang word, try the rubber band reminder.

I have discovered another simple way to raise my awareness of the name of God. (You can include your children in this to help them nurture respect.) Whenever I see a penny on the ground, I stop and pick it up. Every penny is stamped with the declaration "In God We Trust." I know there's nothing magical about picking up a penny, but I just can't leave one behind because I don't want people walking on God's name verbally or with their feet. This is one of the ways I try to stay sensitive to the red flag He waves about His name. If it matters that much to Him, surely it should matter that much to His Smart Girls!

4. Rest Is Not an Optional Thing

God knows so well our tendency to overpack our days that He set aside a period of time for us to be intentional about rest: "Remember to observe the Sabbath day by keeping it holy" (Exod. 20:8). We live in a culture that doesn't know night from day nor the weekend from weekdays. If we don't intentionally seek time to rest and worship and carefully guard that time, it will be stolen away.

Because I speak at women's conferences more than half of the weekends out of the year, I travel on many Sundays. I have to constantly remind myself that a day of rest is important even though I have spent Sunday traveling after ministering on Friday and Saturday. It's so tempting to come home and jump back into the fray of busyness for those few days of the week I'm here before leaving town again. I am easily lulled into thinking I've rested, when in reality I've just exchanged one kind of work for another. Rationalization won't rest my bones; only time set apart to truly relax and change my pace will do that.

There is a spiritual component to God's command to remember the Sabbath day. As New Testament believers, we are not under the law to keep the Sabbath as the Jews were commanded to keep it, but we are not excused from setting aside a time of rest and keeping that day separate. That's what *holy* means: to be separate. Many Christians have adopted the first day of the week, Sunday, as their day of rest, noting that this is the day Jesus rose from the grave as well as the day on which the disciples and the early church gathered to worship. Others, for various reasons, observe Saturday as the Sabbath. Whatever day you set aside to gather with other believers to worship and to rest should be distinctively separate from the activities of your workweek.

> Do not let Sunday be taken from you. . . . If your soul has no Sunday, it becomes an orphan.[1]
>
> —ALBERT SCHWEITZER

We Americans have not been attentive to this red flag and are the poorer for it. When I was a child, I was not allowed to attend birthday parties on Sunday afternoon, I wasn't allowed to go to movies on Sunday afternoon, and no one at our house cut the grass or washed a car on Sunday afternoon. We went to church on Sunday morning, rested in the afternoon, and went back to church on Sunday evening. How rare is that today? I certainly don't advocate a rigid, legalistic perspective on this, but I do believe God knows we need a break from the hectic pace of day-to-day life, a time when anything that smacks of work is set aside in favor of those things that point to God and bring us rest.

The red flag of Sabbath waves for the benefit of every believer because God knows that observing it will refresh us in body and spirit to start the new week.

5. There's No Such Thing as a Perfect Parent—or a Perfect Child

God instructs us to "honor your father and mother" (Exod. 20:12) because this is such a sensitive area in everyone's life, whether we like to admit it or not. The fact that God felt the need to include this in His ten major red flags obviously means it is a problem for more than one of us!

The parent-child relationship is not always smooth. Parents can be wrong and hurtful without even realizing it. Sometimes they do know and just choose to be mean. Deliberate or not, a parent's words and actions can result in torn relationships and broken hearts. Adult children often find themselves wrestling with the question of how to honor their parents after receiving such piercing wounds.

Without a doubt, the red flag against dishonoring our parents needs to be heeded whether or not there is ever reconciliation. God included no caveats that let us off the hook if our parents fail at being good or kind. The responsibility to speak and act with honor rests fully on the child.

All too often, however, adult children misunderstand what it means to honor their parents. They are drawn into being manipulated, controlled, and emotionally batted about because that's all they have known in the relationship. Under the false notion that continuing to tolerate the abusive behavior is a necessary part of honoring their parents, they make themselves vulnerable, hoping against hope that somehow the relationship will be healed.

Some people are tempted to dishonor their parents by talking disrespectfully about them—or to them—and abandoning them to their own stuff; others feel compelled to be subservient to their parents' deviant desires. God's verdict is "Avoid the extremes!" Honor them and take care of their needs. That's all He commands us to do. Honoring our parents does not mean allowing our lives to be entangled with emotionally warped people; rather it requires a conscious act of helping parents when they are in need because it is right.

Jesus spoke clearly about God's heart in this matter. He pointed out to the Pharisees that they were causing trouble for people who wanted to honor their parents by insisting that they give their money to the religious projects of the day.

> Moses gave you this law from God: "Honor your father and mother," and "Anyone who speaks disrespectfully of father or mother must be put to death." But you say it is all right for people to say to their parents, "Sorry, I can't help you. For I have vowed to give to God what I would have given to you." In this way, you let them disregard their needy parents. And so you cancel the word of God in order to hand down your own tradition. (Mark 7:10–13)

Those who want to honor their difficult parents often feel guilty because they don't have warm, fuzzy feelings about their relationships. This much I know: God would never put us under condemnation by telling us to do the impossible and then standing back to watch us fail. It's just not His way. He has placed a red flag in this area to say, "Heads up! Walk carefully here." Take care of your parents in their need, but don't become ensnared with them in the kind of arguments that could give you chronic heartburn.

6. Life Is Not to Be Treated Casually

"You must not murder" (Exod. 20:13) is one of several red flags that may seem incredibly obvious, but here as elsewhere, our all-knowing, all-wise God is trying to open our eyes to a deeper truth. The Hebrew word translated here as *murder* means "to dash in pieces."[2] It refers to the killing of a human being with forethought and intent. Most of us will never stand trial for the physical murder of another human being, but how many of us have wished someone were dead because of what they've done to us or to someone we love? Jesus said that those who harbor such anger are just as guilty as if they'd committed murder (Matt. 5:21–22). If you ever have wanted to kill someone, even if you haven't followed through, you have essentially committed murder in your heart.

Here's what God says to Smart Girls who want to handle tough situations in the right way:

> Never pay back evil with more evil. Do things in such a way that everyone can see you are honorable. Do all that you can to live in peace with everyone.
>
> Dear friends, never take revenge. Leave that to the righteous anger of God. For the Scriptures say, "I will take revenge; I will pay them back," says the LORD.
>
> Instead, "If your enemies are hungry, feed them. If they are thirsty, give them something to drink. In doing this, you will heap burning coals of shame on their heads."
>
> Don't let evil conquer you, but conquer evil by doing good. (Rom. 12:17–21)

Emotional murder is more destructive to the one who plots it than to the intended victim, who may never know he or she is on your emotional hit list. Smart Girls think twice about getting even, knowing there is no beauty in revenge.

One more thing about this red flag: since God makes it unmistakably clear that the premeditated taking of any human life is murder, Smart Girls need to take a stand against the killing of unborn children. I don't want to belabor this issue, but I do think we would do well to be aware of the stakes. My friend Bobbie speaks often of "the two children I killed." At the time, she had no idea that she was actually murdering her babies; she thought she was just handling a problem. But if a friend had been able to point out to her God's red flag of warning draped over that abortion clinic, there would be two precious, grown children in her family today. The good news is that she now knows the truth, has received God's forgiveness, and does not hold on to her regret. Her hope now is to help other women avoid the same mistake.

7. Guard Your Heart

In Exodus 20:14 we find the straightforward caution: "You must not commit adultery." *Adultery* means "having sexual relations with anyone who is not your mate." The same word in the New Testament is inclusive of all unlawful sexual activity. Too many women rationalize promiscuous behavior by saying, "We're consenting adults, and we aren't hurting anyone because neither of us is married." Doesn't matter. God has said that any sexual intercourse outside the bonds of marriage is wrong. Despite what some may claim, He's not out to ruin your fun; He waves this red flag to signal the grave consequences of sharing intimacy outside of marriage.

One of my friends has played the role of the *other woman*. She readily admits to having seen the red flags but choosing to dash past them because she didn't want to give up the man. Despite knowing about her lover's multiple infidelities, she ended up marrying him. A few years into the marriage, he ran off to deceive and seduce another series of women. My friend is all the wiser now, and she is quick to confess that her impulsiveness and sin caused her losses on many levels.

But the dangers of adultery aren't limited to engaging in illicit physical intimacy; in fact, it can be even more difficult to walk away from an affair of the heart. One of the closet secrets of which we rarely speak is emotional adultery committed between women. Sometimes it leads to sexual involvement and becomes a full-blown affair, but more often it is an emotional substitute for intimacy with a husband. This problem of emotional dependency or codependency can ensnare both single and married women.

> Caution is the eldest child of wisdom.
>
> —VICTOR HUGO

Some of the danger signals to watch for in any relationship, whether with a man or a woman, include:

- *Too close too soon.* New friendships occasionally become way too chummy way too soon. If you feel uncomfortable with some of the details your friend is sharing from the heart—or is perhaps pressuring you to reveal—listen carefully to those red-flag emotions.

- *Romanticism.* Some people hold an unrealistic view of what makes a healthy relationship, believing that it's possible to achieve a never-dying, always perfect, totally satisfying relationship. When these dreamy ideas prove unattainable, the dream is threatened, and anger sets in.

- *Exclusivity.* Possessiveness often sneaks into relationships that progress too rapidly toward emotional intimacy. If you have a sense of being confined or trapped in the relationship, or if the other person grows angry when you spend time with others, it's time to consider getting out—fast.

Each of these red flags indicates that a friendship is carrying you into dangerous territory, whether toward a one-sided infatuation or toward potential emotional or physical adultery. Beware and do whatever it takes to guard your heart.

Part of defending our hearts against the dangers of adultery includes guarding our minds and our eyes. The Scriptures instruct our menfolk to think twice about where they rest their eyes. Jesus said, "You have heard the commandment that says, 'You must not commit adultery.' But I say, anyone who even looks at a woman with lust has already committed adultery with her in his heart" (Matt. 5:27–28). The same red-flag warning applies to us. We can't keep on looking at a fine specimen of manhood without committing adultery in our hearts. An appreciative glance is one thing. A lingering look that allows our minds to take us places we only should go with our husbands is quite another.

Smart Girls recognize the pitfalls of romance novels, sex-oriented magazine articles, and sexually explicit movies and television programs. They know that such things promise fulfillment but only create frustration and bring condemnation. We who love the Lord can't afford to even casually wander down these titillating lanes.

8. "Finders Keepers" Is a Crummy Rule

One of the earliest lessons of childhood is not to take something that doesn't belong to you, so we might be tempted to move quickly past the command "You must not steal" (Exod. 20:15), thinking we're fully in the clear. But stealing takes so many subtle forms, and I encourage you to examine carefully your choices in this area. Sensitivity to the small things will keep us sensitive to the big things. If you've been undercharged for a product from the grocery store and went back to pay the difference, you already have thought twice about the demoralizing effects of stealing. That shows you are becoming a well-established Smart Girl in so many ways.

Of course, stealing is not always about money. It can include stealing an employer's time at work while you play on the computer, linger on a personal call, or take a sick day when you aren't sick. There are so many little ways that we tend to justify stealing from work. An hour here or an hour there may not mean much to you, but for an employer, each hour represents debits from his payroll account, money spent without any return on his investment.

Stealing can take even more subtle forms in our relationships and often reveals our selfishness. We don't owe our time to the people we love, but if we choose to spend it on the things we want to do rather than enjoying our family, then we rob our mates and children of our presence and affection. When we greedily hoard our time and resources even though we know our mate or children want our attention, that is stealing.

> No legacy is so rich as honesty.[3]
> —WILLIAM SHAKESPEARE

Observing this red flag requires a deliberate but simple choice. If I know something isn't mine, then I will not take it. If I become aware that something I have isn't mine, such as God's money in my bank account, then I will immediately correct the situation by turning it over to its rightful owner. "Thou shalt not steal" goes way beyond the obvious to shine a spotlight on our very character.

9. Don't Get Caught in a Web of Deception

Stealing is first cousin to lying, another of God's big red flags: "You must not testify falsely against your neighbor" (Exod. 20:16). A person who will lie to you also will steal from you, and one who will steal will also lie.

Lying undermines every relationship it touches. When someone lies, it reveals a lack of respect for a holy God who says "thou shalt not lie," a lack of respect for the person lied to, and a lack of respect for the relationship. I have heard people excuse lying by saying, "Well, it would have killed her to hear the truth, so I just told her a little white lie." Of course, we know there's no such thing. A lie is a lie, and even a *little* one is as potent as a drop of poison in a gallon of milk. A lie will destroy trust, will corrupt character, and will make future relationships rocky. One lie can create enough suspicion to take down the strongest of friendships. One lie from a parent can leave enough questions in the heart of a child to cause him to doubt himself for the rest of his life. One lie from a teenager can shake the confidence of the most trusting parent.

There is just no good lie because the source of all lies is the enemy of our souls. Jesus confronted some liars in His life with these words: "You belong to your father the devil, and you want to do what he wants. He was a murderer from the beginning and was against the truth, because there is no truth in him. When he tells a lie, he shows what he is really like, because he is a liar and the father of lies" (John 8:44 NCV).

God posted red flags against lying and stealing both because they are evil in and of themselves and because they give the enemy a foothold in our lives. Smart Girls can be trusted because they claim this simple motto: "I don't steal anything, and I don't lie about anything. That settles it."

10. Don't Measure Life by the Size of Your Kitchen

When your girlfriend gets a new house or even when she just redecorates, watch out for a red flag waving: "You must not covet your neighbor's house. You must not covet your neighbor's wife [or husband!], male or female servant, ox or donkey, or anything else that belongs to your neighbor" (Exod. 20:17).

I for one know how easy it is to develop a covetous ("I wish that were mine") spirit. I really have to talk to myself, think twice, and choose against being dissatisfied with my house when I visit someone who lives in a designer decorated home. My family home is comfortable, but it's by no means a showcase. So if I'm not on guard against covetousness, my wishes get way overblown and my gratitude level plummets. That's what covetousness does. It sets us up for a restless lack of contentment, and we fail to recognize all the great ways God has shown His goodness to us. Instead of being grateful for what we have, we begin to focus on what we wish we had and a restless longing settles in our hearts.

When we notice dissatisfaction creeping into our lives, we need to realize that it's not really about the neighbor's gorgeous house or her dream job or her generous husband or her overachieving children or her cleaning service or her BMW sports car; the issue actually centers on our heart toward God and whether or not we're going to choose an attitude of gratitude. A thankful heart is always too big and too warm to be wrapped up in a smothering blanket of covetousness.

> The covetous man is ever in want.
>
> —HORACE

Red Flags Are Not There for Decoration

God has placed red flags in danger zones for our good and protection. His loving desire is to keep His people from blundering off into bad decisions and bad habits. Once we've been flagged down, it becomes our job to do something about it. The book of James offers crucial advice for the Smart Girl who has seen God's ten red flags.

> Do what God's teaching says; when you only listen and do nothing, you are fooling yourselves. Those who hear God's teaching and do nothing are like people who look at themselves in a mirror. They see their faces and then go away and quickly forget

what they looked like. But the truly happy people are those who carefully study God's perfect law that makes people free, and they continue to study it. They do not forget what they heard, but they obey what God's teaching says. Those who do this will be made happy. (1:22–25 NCV)

These verses remind me of those cautionary signs we see at gas pumps: "Danger! Explosive gas. No smoking. No open flames within twenty feet." Yet how many times have you seen someone get out of his car with a cigarette in his mouth and start to pump gas? When I see someone so careless about something so dangerous, I know they have little regard for the red flags that are posted for their safety. I guess they figure they've done it before and nothing happened, so why not keep doing it?

> If you wish success in life, make perseverance your bosom friend, experience your wise counselor, caution your elder brother, and hope your guardian genius.
>
> —JOSEPH ADDISON

Sadly, this is the attitude many take toward the warnings God has posted. The rationalization of the human mind is wildly deceptive. We can talk ourselves into and out of doing nearly anything. But Smart Girls know that if God says it, we'd better listen, whether or not we can see the reason for His warning. God's wisdom for us has a certain mark. It is recognizable. "But the wisdom that is from above is first pure, then peaceable, gentle, willing to yield, full of mercy and good fruits, without partiality and without hypocrisy" (James 3:17 NKJV). It is God's heart that we hear and obey what He is saying. He wants His children to know His touch, to recognize His voice. Watching for the warnings and heeding His instructions puts you in a safety zone designed by Him. God smiles when a Smart Girl sees the red flags and then makes the choice to avoid, evade, dodge, elude, shake

off, get out of, do anything possible to get away from the dangerous philosophy, relationship, temptation, or attitude that threatens
her well-being.

Chapter 3

Don't Let Life Slip Away

Smart Girls Think Twice About Time

During a conference in Chattanooga, Tennessee, in 2004, I received a wonderful, creative basket full of treats from the local chamber of commerce. As I prowled through the goodies, enjoying each new find, I spied a pocket calendar. Now this wasn't your average one-year or ten-year calendar. It was a *twenty-year* pocket calendar. My first thought was, *This is cool. I wonder where I can get a dozen of these to give as gifts.* But as I looked through it year by year, a new thought dawned on me, *Twenty years! What on earth will I be doing in twenty years?* How could I, or any one else, think of making an appointment for twenty years from that moment?

Then I got curious and did some calculations. I started from that day and counted the months until my eightieth birthday in 2024, twenty years in the future. I calculated that I had 237 months left until I turned eighty. That rocked me into reality as I thought how quickly twelve months go by, and here I was looking at only 237 of those months. Of course, I realize it all depends on the Lord's timing and plans, but I found this discovery interesting and a bit dismaying. Time cut up in months seems much, much shorter than time laid out in years.

Why don't you try it yourself? Calculate the number of years between now and your eightieth birthday, then multiply by twelve to see about how many months it adds up to. What does that do for your perspective on life? Does it jolt you as much as it did me?

Now, I understand that God could take all of us Home before that time or after, but let's just say you live until you are eighty. How many months do you have left to fully live the life you've been given? How do you think you will use them?

This Is Your Time

"Then God said, 'Let lights appear in the sky to separate the day from the night. Let them mark off the seasons, days, and years'" (Gen. 1:14). God, who is eternal, who has no beginning and no end, thought it important for us to live in increments of time. Daylight and dusk, phases of the moon, and seasons of the year affect our lives in ways we sometimes don't even realize. But God had a purpose in creating the dimension of time.

The psalmist David said of God,

> You saw my body as it was formed.
> All the days planned for me
> were written in your book
> before I was one day old. (Ps. 139:16 NCV)

And Job, the author of the oldest book in the Bible, wrote:

Our time is limited.
You have given us only so many months to live
and have set limits we cannot go beyond. (Job 14:5 NCV)

So time is allotted out to us in certain ways that we know and recognize as well as in ways we won't know and can't discover until our lives are complete. Time is an ongoing commodity, but for each of us it is limited and much of its value is determined by how smart we are in using each given day.

The author of Ecclesiastes observed, "There is an appointed time for everything. And there is a time for every event under heaven" (Eccl. 3:1 NASB). I love those words. They bring such order to my mind. Our days and seasons are not just haphazardly thrown together; they are appointed, they are expected, and they are the canvas on which we draw our lives. Smart Girls love the differing seasons of life. They don't try to hang on to the past, and they don't dread the future. They embrace each day they've been given in any particular season and appreciate it for what it is. In every season, no matter its challenges, you can find something good and you can find ways to enhance your life and the lives of others. Even in those seasons that feel a little uncomfortable, there are lovely, interesting, meaningful, kind things to do until the day we leave this earth.

> Time flies like an arrow; the days and nights alternate as fast as a weaver's shuttle.
>
> —CHINESE PROVERB

I have a bright, energetic friend who recently entered the season of retirement. She has always lived to the max and has accomplished a great deal in her life. Now she is experiencing a different sort of life and is moving at a different pace. With her retired husband home during the day, she's adjusting to a new normal in her routine. Her energy level isn't as high as it used to be, so things she used to do easily now require more effort. Life has taken on an altered rhythm and purpose, but she embraces each day with the same gusto with which she has lived the rest of her life. She continues to be interested in new experiences, taking lessons in ballroom dancing, learning to paint, joining a book club where she met a new set of friends. She knows that for "everything there is a season, [and] a time for every purpose under heaven" (Eccl. 3:1 NKJV). Since she is alive today, this is her time.

And since you and I are alive today, too, this is our time. I remember often hearing as a college student, "These are the best years of your life." I always rolled my eyes and thought, *If these are the best, I'd hate to see the worst.* The pressure of studying, writing term papers, dating, falling in love, sharing a room with two other girls, and having to ride a train four hours both ways when I wanted to go home for the weekend was not my idea of the best years. If I'd been a Smart Girl in that season, I would have studied harder, learned more, relaxed about the future, and soaked up the college experience. But I had no idea that it was a season to embrace. I was only looking forward to the day when I could get on with what I thought of as *real life.* In fact, I took a couple of correspondence courses so I could qualify to graduate early. Why was I rushing like that?

As I look back over other seasons of my life, I feel as if I have wished most of them away as well. I spent so many years thinking about what it would be like *when* . . . What will life be like when I get married? What will it be like when I have children? What will life be like when I have an empty nest? What will it be like when I'm a grandmother? Now I know the answers to all those questions. What life will be like *then* has been revealed, but

> One of the most tragic things I know about human nature is that all of us tend to put off living.[1]
>
> —DALE CARNEGIE

only in the past few years have I stopped thinking about the future and what it will be like. I finally have learned a great truth: when each season comes, it will be what it will be. There is an appointed time for every event yet to occur, and God will be with me in the future just as He has been alongside me all the way, every step, for every event and for every feeling, good or bad. Therefore, whatever time remains on my calendar, I don't want to wish it away. I want to relish it. I finally got smart.

We have today. That's it. We have the joy of yesterday's memories and the delight of future anticipation, but we have no tangible reality except today. This day is yours. This is your time to do, to be, to accomplish, to fulfill your reason for living.

Thinking twice about what you do with today is a Smart Girl's privilege, so I encourage you to take some time to think about your time. What are you doing now? What season are you living in? Have you wished any time away? Do you need to let go of some worries about the future and just leave it to God?

Where Does the Time Go?

One of the reasons we fail to make the most of each day is that we somehow lose track of our time; it's being stolen away from us, and we don't even notice. When you feel stressed and stretched, can't seem to find time to finish what you start, struggle under a load of obligation and guilt, or feel numb and depressed when you think about the day ahead, the *time thieves* have already made their move.

Let's take a look at some of the usual suspects.

Time Thief: The Household Idol

Many of us have lost our time to a thief I call the *household idol*. That term is connected to certain religions whose followers have idols enshrined in their homes. Their practice is to offer food to the idol, and in return they believe it will watch over their domestic matters. Like them, many of us have a household idol that shines unashamedly from its place of enshrinement while we regularly offer it our time and small chunks of our brain cells. You may be thinking, *I have no such thing in my house!* Well, here's what I'm getting at: Do you have a television (or two or three) in your home? Do you frequently give it a sacrifice of your time and brain cells? Do you entrust it with certain domestic matters like keeping the kids quiet or filling your time when you're bored? Not every television is a household idol, but if we don't set careful limits on its use, we'll find ourselves habitually handing over our time to it like religious devotees.

Certainly, there are some wonderful, educational, entertaining programs on television. It can be a great tool for making us smarter, better informed, and more empathetic with the world beyond our doors. It also can make us dumber, falsely informed, and callous to tragedies and traumas in people's lives. We can see only so much blood and tears before it all becomes just another reality show. We can take in only so much fifth-grade humor before we begin to view such rubbish as the standard. We reach the point where we aren't offended anymore and don't even realize that the producers of such drivel are insulting our intelligence and character.

> I find television very educational. Every time someone switches it on, I go into another room and read a good book.[2]
> —GROUCHO MARX

Time is too precious to waste in watching voyeuristic news and foolish entertainment. How much can we stand hearing about the drunken antics or tawdry love lives of celebrities? How many dysfunctional, bitter TV families can we watch insult one another for the sake of laughs? How many *extreme* adventures will we follow religiously while missing the extreme adventure of our own lives? Smart Girls have to think twice and make a choice. How much time will you offer up to the household idol in the corner?

Time Thief: Techie Toys

I love my BlackBerry and my computer and my cell phone and all things technical. I also know that these shiny little techie toys have a way of stealing my days, one minute at a time. Precious moments are so easily frittered away when we become absorbed with our latest gadget. Unless we set deliberate limits for ourselves, we always seem to spend more time than we think we will in answering e-mails, surfing the Internet, fiddling with our settings, and even sometimes playing those cool but addictive games.

Computer games can be fun and relaxing when you need a little break, but if they're taking time away from family, from work, from fulfilling obligations, you need to Stop, Look, Listen, and Look Again at what this use of your time reveals. Computer games sometimes serve as a distraction from reality, a means of numbing emotional pain. I believe that anyone who is truly enjoying life will be unwilling to give up too much of their time for gaming. If you find yourself frequently slipping away from the company of others so you can play solitaire, you need to think twice about seeking some help to regain your joy for life.

Technology is here to stay, and I love all of its conveniences (how did we ever get by without cell phones?), but Smart Girls know the human touch is far more important than time spent with computer chips and monitors. They muster the discipline to shut off the cell phone, power down the BlackBerry, and turn off the computer in order to focus on the people in their lives. They also know that these thieves can steal away our time with God. He loves to spend time with us and invites us to come into His presence, but it is, oh, so easy to get detoured by one of our techie toys. Would a Smart Girl rob God?

Time Thief: Mental Escape

Computer games, television, and other activities can serve as wonderful mental breaks, giving us time to wind down from the demands of life. But like anything else, we have to set reasonable limits; otherwise those harmless mental escapes can become vicious time thieves.

For example, many of us find shopping to be a relaxing diversion. The wonders of chocolate or mashed potatoes can't compare with the endorphins released when you find a kickin' new pair of shoes—on sale! Wandering through department stores, touching, feeling, dreaming, and occasionally buying can feel good for the moment, but it also can numb your mind and soul. Again let me say, a little shopping is great. A girl has to get some new clothes or a little bling every now and then. But when it becomes a way to *kill time* or turns into an obsessive compulsion that consumes money you don't have on trinkets you don't need, a Smart Girl will think twice about healthy ways to invest her time rather than throwing it away on more stuff.

Romance novels also seem to have a mind-killing addictive power that draws you into a world where time has no reality. They're all about killing time or wishing it away on a fantasy. In fact,

> Dost thou love life? Then do not squander time, for that is the stuff life is made of.
> —BENJAMIN FRANKLIN

anything we do just to kill time—even essentially healthy activities like reading, chatting on the phone, or completing a sudoku puzzle—becomes a time thief. It's one thing to take a few minutes to relax, but why on earth would we want to kill time? A commodity so limited and precious deserves more respect. If you ever catch yourself thinking, *I'll just kill some time*, think again; that's not something any of us really wants to do.

Time Thief: Misguided Sense of Obligation

The trademark tool of this thief is a clamoring insistence that you answer every question and say yes to every request. If you're a southern girl like me, you're well acquainted with how quickly a misguided sense of obligation can consume your time. You've been taught that hospitality is paramount and that making a person feel warm in your presence is your duty. "Sugar, you be nice to everyone you meet. It's impolite not to speak. It's rude not to ask people in when they come to the door."

Protecting your time against this thief is extremely difficult. So often the people we feel obligated to be involved with are neighbors, friends, or even family members. Of course, we need and want to be involved in such relationships, but occasionally we find ourselves trapped rather than enjoying our time together, which is why we need to figure out how to extricate ourselves when necessary. Each of us lives by a different timetable, but not everyone recognizes those differences. Smart Girls know they need to think twice before setting their boundaries and then stick to them. If done graciously, people will understand.

When I was a young army wife, I lived in a community with young mothers. Fourteen of us had new babies during the eight months our husbands were in helicopter pilot training school. We all lived in close proximity to the post, so visiting back and forth was a regular part of our days. We could care for our babies and encourage one another while our men were away.

One of the girls seemed to enjoy visiting more than the others. Inevitably, when I had plans for the day, I would look out the front window and see her pushing her baby stroller up my front walk. She always had a big pile of diapers and bottles in the storage basket of the stroller, which meant she was set to spend the day at my place. I loved her company and I loved her sweet baby, but we weren't working from the same timetable. A Smart Girl would have set some limits on her availability, but I didn't know how to do that back then. If a similar situation occurred today, I would meet her at the door and say, "Oh, I didn't know you were free today. I've already made plans, and I'm going to have to pass on getting together. Give me a call next time, and I'll see if I can work it out." Responses like that put you in control of your time— without being rude.

Learning how to set boundaries graciously helps ensure that relationships are preserved along with your time. How we choose to use our time is such a personal issue, and we all handle it differently, so helping others to understand what will work and what won't work for you is a delicate art. But this is one of those "Do unto others as you would have them do unto you" areas. If you were stepping on someone's time and didn't know it, how would you want to be told?

Investing Your Time Where It Counts

Most of us can be much more effective in choosing when to say yes and when to say no by focusing on those activities that draw on our strengths and passions. Some great tests are available online to help you to find out what your gifting is and what your strengths may be, if you haven't discovered them already. One of my favorite tests is at Strengthsfinder.com. I like it because it doesn't dwell on what you can't do but rather emphasizes what you can do. I would highly recommend that every growing Smart Girl make it her aim to know what she does best. Then make that the basis on which you arrange your time commitments.

After I discovered what God had wired me to do best, I took a closer look at my passions, the things that matter to me above all else. I made several lists and inevitably the top five loves of my life appeared every time. Now that I understand how God designed me, I find it very easy to say no to requests that lie outside my strengths and passions—and exhilarating to say yes to programs and projects that are a good fit. My schedule is not so cluttered with obligatory *yeses*, which leaves more room for the true yeses of my heart. This doesn't mean that other things I am asked to do are not worthy; it's just that I realize I have only so much time and I am passionate about using it for the things God has given me to throw myself into.

> What I do today is important because I am exchanging a day of my life for it.
>
> —FROM "A NEW DAY" BY HEARTSILL WILSON

Effective Time Management Can Save a Relationship

I believe a Smart Girl would never knowingly steal someone's time any more than she would steal someone's money. The key word in that statement is *knowingly*; part of being smart is being sensitive to the concerns of others and aware of the ways we may unintentionally steal their time. A Smart Girl knows that being trustworthy with time is part of the fulfillment of her life's calling. When she says she'll be somewhere at a certain time, the people who are counting on her need to be confident that she will be there.

If, however, people typically have to wait on you or if friends jokingly comment on your habitual tardiness, maybe there's a time issue you need to address. If you are really smart, you'll listen to what they say, and more than likely you'll recognize that the joking isn't so funny. In fact, it may signal a crisis in your friendship.

Unfortunately, routine lateness broadcasts the message, "I'm more important than you are." Whether or not that is how you feel, if you're tardy on a regular basis, that is the message you're sending. Good manners look attractive on anybody, and punctuality is a vital aspect of etiquette.

The person who finds herself waiting too often for a friend is in a tough position if she wants to have integrity in the use of her own time and also maintain the relationship. When the wait is only a few minutes, most friends don't mind being patient. But when someone arrives more than ten or fifteen minutes late on a regular basis, there's a problem that needs to be addressed before the relationship suffers irreparable damage.

I have a sweet friend who isn't as attuned to promptness as I am, so after a few disappointments and a little frustration (on both sides, I'm sure), I said, "Let's make a deal for whenever we get together: if you set the appointment, we'll go on your timetable, but if I initiate the date, we'll go on mine, which is 'on time.'" We agreed and each of us has been satisfied with that arrangement ever since.

So being a Smart Girl doesn't mean being legalistic and hard nosed. It means that you appreciate the value of reaching an understanding about many things, including time. Too few people talk directly about such problems. If someone in your life has decided that late is okay, then you can choose how you will conduct yourself. If late is not okay with you, then it's up to you to remedy the situation. If that means ordering dinner and eating alone until your late companion arrives, so be it. If driving separately to an event is your remedy, that's fine. If you give notice that you'll leave the appointed place after a fifteen-minute wait, that's okay too. The point is, you have identified the issue, have presented solutions, and are willing to stand by your plan. It may cause a bit of dismay the first time or two you implement the arrangement, but I believe in most cases it will bring you and the tardy party to a more positive resolution than if you had allowed the lateness to continue without intervention.

A Smart Girl knows that she can't force others to conform to her priorities; she can only tend to her own time, but she can do so with grace and integrity.

Ultimately, Time Is in God's Hands

Just as your use of time reflects your character, God has defined Himself through His use of time. One of the ways He has verified to us that He is truly God is by the messages given through His prophets, including 333 prophecies about the first coming of Jesus Christ. Every one of those prophecies was fulfilled in time and on time, just as God put it in the hearts of His prophets to prophesy. Hebrews 1:1–2 sums it up like this: "God, after He spoke long ago to the fathers in the prophets in many portions and in many ways, in these last days has spoken to us in His Son, whom He appointed heir of all things, through whom also He made the world" (NASB).

Look at the two time phrases in these verses: *long ago* and *these last days*. Long ago, God said certain things would happen. Those prophecies were given BC (before Christ). They were completed when Jesus was born in Bethlehem of Judea and walked the earth for thirty-three years. Now in these last days (the days after Christ came), we are living in the fulfillment of God's prophecies AD.

What difference does it make? Well, maybe it doesn't seem like a big deal on a day-to-day basis, but the very fact that God said it and it was so tells us that He is a faithful God who fulfills—on time—everything that He speaks and all that He desires. That includes what He wants to accomplish in our lives.

A big stressor for women seems to be the inability to rest in the fact that God is in control and that He knows the times and seasons in our lives. Smart Girls, however, think twice when they are tempted to worry or to force life to move at their pace. They realize that God moves according to His sovereignty, not according to our timetable, and they have learned to trust His timing in every area of life. When you grasp the truth that He is in control and that when He moves it will be according to His perfect plan, it makes a huge difference in your life.

When you waste time worrying about what door is going to open next or you are constantly asking questions like, "When is Mr. Right going to come along?" or "When will I get the promotion I deserve?" or "What will happen if my biological clock runs out before I get pregnant?" you aren't trusting that God is in control. When you do trust Him, those questions may still trip through your head, but you surrender them to God, knowing He is the one who started your heart beating and He is the one who will stop it. In between those moments you can say with the psalmist, "But as for me, I trust in You, O LORD; I say, 'You are my God.' My times are in Your hand" (Ps. 31:14–15 NKJV).

> Next time you're disappointed, don't panic. Don't jump out. Don't give up. Just be patient and let God remind you he's still in control.[3]
>
> —MAX LUCADO

God is the God of all times, and to know Him is to know Faithfulness itself. He has the big picture in mind, and He knows the plans He has for you. Your times are safe in His hand. There is no need to be anxious about when God is going to answer your prayer or move on your behalf. You can relax in the certainty that His ways and His timing are perfect. Keep in mind there is a "time for everything" and the last chapter hasn't yet been written!

Trusting God to be God is one of the greatest attributes of a Smart Girl. In fact, that's what makes you smart!

Chapter 4

Checks and Balances

Smart Girls Think Twice About Money

Counting paper money and coins always makes my hands feel dirty. There's no telling where that cash has traveled or whose hands it has passed through. And yet money is one of the absolute necessities of life. You can't get too far without it.

Although many of us have a love-hate relationship with it, the truth is that money, in and of itself, is neither evil nor good. Money is completely amoral. It has no conscience. Our attitude toward money is what makes all the difference. For those who love money, this inanimate object holds a seductive attraction and arouses deep emotion. Some individuals abuse money and then suddenly find the tables turned as they become its victim. In the right hands, money creates power and prestige, but often it sifts quickly through their fingers or wraps around their hearts, in both cases creating wretchedness and ruin. As the Scriptures say, "For the love of money is the root of all kinds of evil. And some people, craving money, have wandered from the true faith and pierced themselves with many sorrows" (1 Tim. 6:10).

Control Your Money or It Will Control You

Jesus knows human hearts and the way money affects us. In talking with His followers, He observed, "No one can serve two masters. Either he will hate the one and love the other, or he will be devoted to the one and despise the other. You cannot serve both God and Money" (Matt. 6:24 NIV). The word He used here for money—*mammōnas* in Aramaic, His language—means "that in which one trusts."[1] In other words, we can place our confidence in God or in money, but not both.

Smart Girls know that when it comes to money matters, they need to think twice about their perspective. Whatever money we have comes

> Those who love money will never have enough. How meaningless to think that wealth brings true happiness!
> —ECCLESIASTES 5:10

from God and is meant to be managed, not worshiped. If we have money, any amount of money, we are required to become stewards, responsible to God for its use. We are not to reverence it, nor are we to ignore it and just hope everything will come out even in the end.

The way you manage money reflects how well you manage life. That's a bold statement but it's true. When you see a person who is smart about her money in every way, not greedy and in love with it but wise about how she relates to it, you'll find a person who is doing well in life. I'm not saying she'll be well-to-do. I am speaking rather of the person who has found a way to live within her means and has learned to be content with what she has. That's what it means to live well.

Luci Swindoll is a woman with a vast store of wisdom and insight. When she was a little girl, her father told her that there were five things she needed to do when she earned or received money. He assured her that if she did those things she always would have money. Luci has followed his advice all her life and says his five principles for handling money have held her in good standing all the way. Here they are:

1. Spend some
2. Save some
3. Tithe some
4. Invest some
5. Give some away

I believe any Smart Girl could pick up that pattern for handling money and know what to do with every cent that comes through her hands. I've tucked that one in my brain, and I recommend that you file it away as well. (Okay, our brains may not be the best place. Maybe you can tuck it away on a three-by-five-inch index card instead.)

Money Matters in Relationships

Money is often an extremely sensitive topic, especially in marriages. In fact, a 2006 survey found that 84 percent of respondents cited money as a cause of tension in their marriages.[2]

My own sweet husband and I looked at money from totally different perspectives when we first married. I have to confess it has taken me longer to become a Smart Girl about money than about many other issues in my life. I always have hated to keep track of it. In fact I used to call the meticulous accounting mentality of balancing a checkbook to the last penny "the hobgoblin of little minds." And I married an engineer who thinks balancing the checkbook is a high-priority activity! You only can imagine how much fun it was at our house when bill-paying-and-checkbook-balancing time came around. It certainly wasn't pretty.

My remedy was finally to get my own checkbook. That may sound radical, but I assure you it only brought peace to our home. I kept track of what I spent from my checkbook. There wasn't much in there, but at least I knew I was responsible for it and somehow that was the impetus I needed to stay on top of my spending. I still don't like the task of reconciling my checkbook, but I do it because I know it has to be done.

> If a person gets his attitude toward money right, it will help straighten out almost every other area of his life.[3]
>
> —BILLY GRAHAM

I'm not suggesting that as the answer for every woman, but it worked for me. Whatever works for you and enables you to be responsible for your money is what you need to do. Accounting for your money is like keeping up with nuclear materials: failure to know exactly what you have and where it's going can bring disastrous results—including explosive arguments with those affected by your choices.

Of course, money and the things it buys can not only cause rifts between husband and wife but can split entire families, especially when an estate is divided after the death of a parent or grandparent. The fighting that goes on over money and possessions is a legacy no one would knowingly leave. Yet sometimes it happens anyway. I've seen sisters estranged for life over a few hundred dollars and a little jewelry. I've seen daughters left in a world of pain because a parent failed to leave a will and they couldn't figure out how to please everyone in dividing up the estate.

Smart Girls know they are responsible to supervise their money all the way to their deaths. They don't just assume that money will administrate itself after they are gone. They take care of it ahead of time because they recognize its power to destroy and divide. Writing out a will may not be the most pleasant task because it reminds us of our immortality, but it's not difficult to do, and it demonstrates thoughtful consideration for those you leave behind.

My friend Debbie carried out one of the kindest acts someone could do for her friends. At only forty-nine years old, she was losing a five-year battle with breast cancer. When it became obvious that she would not live much longer, this single woman thoughtfully divided the money in her estate among her close friends. I was humbled to learn that she had left me some money. It got me through a dry time in my finances. Debbie had planned ahead and determined that her friends would receive what she wanted them to have. She could have avoided the whole issue, but she didn't. She chose to be a steward of God's gifts even unto death.

Discover the Benefits of Delayed Gratification

Keeping a healthy perspective on what we don't have can be just as challenging as properly handling what we do have. How many times have you looked into the eyes of a child asking you to spend money on a treat and felt tempted to say yes when you knew that saying no would be more to his benefit? In a consumer culture where kids are exposed to so many demands for their attention, it's hard to teach the joys of delayed gratification. They rarely see it as a joy when you turn down their requests and give them the chance to practice contentment; but trust me, when they become adults, you both will be glad you made the effort to help them understand that delayed gratification brings payoffs that will bless them beyond measure.

Children who fail to learn the lessons of delayed gratification grow into adults with a dangerous sense of entitlement that can rarely be overcome without a good deal of pain. Patricia is such an adult. Her parents didn't have a lot of money, and what they did have wasn't handled well. So Patricia arrived at adulthood convinced that she had missed out on a lot of things, and she saw no reason to wait until she had the money to buy them. She reasoned that if she held off buying until she had saved up enough, she might never get what she wanted. Her faulty logic landed her in a pit of financial trouble. It took a lot of pain for her to realize that she was addicted to spending, driven to get the stuff she'd never had but wanted so very much.

> Money cannot purchase what the heart desires.
> —CHINESE PROVERB

Delayed gratification is a matter of trust. If you can trust God to hold something for you until He provides the money to buy it, there will be no doubt when the time comes that the item was meant to be yours. That kind of trust means that you never hedge your bets by assuming He wants you to have something and therefore buying it on credit even though you can't pay it off.

If you talk to God about something important that you think you need, He's not going to hold out on you. If He knows it is truly in your best interest, why would He not gladly give it to you? Jesus assured His followers:

> Ask, and it will be given to you; seek, and you will find; knock, and it will be opened to you. For everyone who asks receives, and he who seeks finds, and to him who knocks it will be opened. Or what man is there among you who, if his son asks for bread, will give him a stone? Or if he asks for a fish, will he give him a serpent? If you then, being evil, know how to give good gifts

to your children, how much more will your Father who is in heaven give good things to those who ask Him! (Matt. 7:7–11 NKJV)

Trusting God and being willing to earn the money ahead of time are the two pillars of delayed gratification. It's not easy, but when these principles guide your spending habits, you will avoid self-induced financial trouble. And let me add, living like this does not mean your desires won't ever be gratified; it just means that when you finally do get what you thought you wanted, you'll still want it and appreciate it. So many things we buy on impulse simply don't taste good, feel good, or smell good once we get them home.

I weep for the child at the grocery store checkout whose mother caves to demands for candy just to gain herself a little peace. The moment she sighs and gives in, her child has learned to circumvent delayed gratification. The lesson learned is "pitch a fit and you can have what you want." If that becomes a habitual practice, the problems ahead—for both mother and child—are many. Spoiled children become spoiled teenagers, and spoiled teens become young adults with a sense of entitlement. If your children have never heard *no* and *wait* from you—or if they don't observe you regularly practicing self-control—then they will have a hard time dealing with teachers and employers and life. Smart Girls understand the benefits of delayed gratification and pass them on.

Lending Money Is Risky Business

The need to know when to say no when it comes to money extends beyond our children and ourselves. When someone asks you to loan her money, remember the principles of Stop, Look, Listen, and Look Again. Stop and consider your motive in lending. Look closely at her motive for asking. Listen for what your instincts are telling you. Think twice about how this might affect your relationship. Ask yourself some penetrating questions: Are you seeking the borrower's approval? Can you say no just as evenly as you can say yes? Do you expect the borrower to pay you back? Will you be able to stay solvent if she doesn't repay? How will borrowing affect your relationship?

Smart Girls know that lending or borrowing money is a risky business. Ben Franklin, known for his wise sayings, said, "Neither a borrower nor a lender be." He knew the risks and apparently had determined that the best thing a person could do was to avoid the transaction altogether. Of course, Ben was a wily old fox, not known for his graciousness. Jesus, on the other hand, the very embodiment of grace and truth, said, "But love your enemies, and do good, and lend, expecting nothing in return; and your reward will be great, and you will be sons of the Most High" (Luke 6:35 NASB). For Jesus, who knows and loves us, it's all about the attitude behind the lending. He spoke of lending to enemies and of giving without expecting anything in return.

I determined a long time ago that I would never lend money but if someone came to me with a need, and I had the money, I would give it. My creed is "I won't lend it to you, but I will give it to you." I have seen too many people lend and live to resent it. I also have seen too many people borrow money and fail to repay, leaving a trail of bitterness in their wake.

Lending money needs to be guided by wisdom. If someone is borrowing money to support a habit, you do them no good by lending them money. If you are asked to lend money for an unethical project, no is the only answer you can give.

But when the need is genuine, we do well to seriously consider our response. Psalm 37:26 states that the righteous "are always generous and lend freely" (NIV), and God frequently warns His people against charging interest when they lend money to those in need. But the Scriptures also say that cosigning for a loan is unwise: "It's poor judgment to guarantee another person's debt or put up security for a friend" (Prov. 17:18). If you cannot lend freely or give outright, you're wise to avoid the pitfall of cosigning and becoming responsible for another person's debt.

Giving Credit Its Due

Speaking of loans and debt, there's no faster way to get into money trouble than to mess up your credit. Your credit rating either will bless you or curse you when you try to do business in our economy. Like it or not, it's practically impossible to function financially these days without credit.

I remember being shocked when, as a young married couple, we tried to buy a washer and dryer set from Sears. They said we couldn't buy it on credit because we had no credit. I thought, *No credit? We've been married four years, he has served in the army for three years, and we just bought a house with a GI loan.* But in their estimation we didn't have credit! It was a mystery to me until I realized you have to take deliberate steps to establish credit; you have to prove your financial responsibility. So from that day on, we worked to establish credit, little by little, by purchasing small things on a credit card and paying them off immediately. We figured out early on that credit is just one of those things you have to have. Without it you can't buy a car or rent an apartment or take out a loan for college.

That Magic Piece of Plastic

These days everyone also needs a credit card, if only to rent a car, reserve a hotel room, or buy an airline ticket. But one of the best lessons any girl can learn is that a credit card is a convenience, not an entitlement. Once you have access to a credit card, it all becomes a matter of self-control. If you have a personal rule that you will never put more on a credit card than you can honestly pay at the end of the month, it will be one of the smartest things you can do. If you can't pay it off each due date, you'll find that compounded interest, the details of which are hidden in the fine print on the back of your statement, will begin to show up on the front in nice bold type in the form of extra charges. Credit card companies are not sugar daddies handing out loans because they like you and want you to have what you want when you want it. They are businesses, and they profit from your urge to overspend. Every time you take advantage of the convenience of their little plastic card, you are in bondage to them until you pay it off.

I have to laugh now about a time when credit card trouble caused more than a little upset in our household, though it was all an innocent mistake on my part. My daddy, who was elderly and sick at the time, asked me to pick out an anniversary gift for my mother. He wanted me to get her a nice ring. He would give me a check to cover the cost in a few weeks when I brought him the ring to give to Mother. I found a gorgeous ring with diamonds and sapphires and a lovely setting, charged it to our personal credit card (the only one we had), and thought nothing more about it. I knew my daddy had the money and would pay me as soon as I saw him. Innocent enough, right?

A couple of weeks later I received a phone call from my sweet husband, who was out of town on a trip. His voice was not filled with warmth and joy. "I need you to send me money by Western Union so I can have a place to stay tonight." I thought, *What on earth is this about?* He explained that when he tried to check into his hotel, he was refused because the credit card he presented was maxed out. "Maxed out?" I can only imagine his surprise. We had never maxed out our credit card, and he made it a practice to pay the full balance due every month. He knew he hadn't charged any large items, so I was the next most likely culprit. Oops! I explained to him about the ring and said I'd go straight to Western Union, which I did. He had to wait quite awhile to check into the hotel. I thought at the time, *It's probably best that he is several states away.* Trust me, I thought twice from then on about any purchase I put on our card, even if I knew it could be paid off immediately.

On Time, Every Time

One of the best tips for keeping good credit is to pay on time. When I first started managing money, I lived under the mistaken notion that as long as a bill was postmarked on the due date, all would be well. I found out it took more than a postmark to make things good with the billing department. If they said they wanted their payment on the twenty-first of the month, they wanted it in their hands, on their desk, recorded in their computer on that day! If the mail was late, even if it was postmarked on the nineteenth, it was really too bad but they'd be charging me a late fee. Getting my payment there in a timely fashion was not their problem; it was mine. Smart Girls soon learn that keeping up with the due dates on bills is as important as sending in the money. (Well, maybe not *as* important, but it surely does matter.)

Paying bills isn't just about avoiding late fees and preserving your credit; paying on time is a reflection of your character, much like being on time for an appointment. To pay a bill on time reflects your respect for the person you owe. Failure to pay in a timely way says, "I have more important issues to deal with." Smart Girls pay on time, every time whether they're sending a check to a big company or returning a five-dollar loan from a friend. They do it because it's the right thing to do.

Where Did All This Stuff Come From?

Smart Girls think twice not only about how to deal with money but also about what to do with all the things it buys. *Stuff* is the sum total of all the things that we have around us. All of it costs money, and, at some point in time, we thought it would enhance our lives. As I look around my office right now, I see stuff that seemed important when I bought it, but at this moment it seems to be in the way. In fact, it not only seems to be in the way, it *is* in the way. I have to move it, dust it, move it again to make room for something else, and then dust the spot where it sat. That's just one of the ways stuff gradually takes over our lives.

I flipped on a television program yesterday on which a man demonstrating the latest in sunglasses said, "Of course, you have to have a new style of sunglasses every year." That struck me as a *stuff* statement. Where is it written that we have to have a new pair of sunglasses every year?

Money paves the way for us to get and to give various things in life, but if we fall for lines such as "you have to have this," then we mindlessly give up that leverage in order to buy something we may not even want in order to comply with someone else's expectation.

I consider myself a fairly Smart Girl, but in this area I know I need to think twice more often. I am far too influenced by my perceived need for more instead of my confidence in what I have. Every year, I clean out my closet and pass on the clothes I no longer wear. I'm sometimes surprised at all of the shirts and blouses I thought I needed. I really only wear four or five outfits during a season, so a whole closet full of stuff is unnecessary. The clothes that I rarely wear are just money on a hanger. When I think of them that way, it helps me resist the temptation to bring home every cute little sale item I find.

Intentionally cutting down on the stuff in my life is my desire. Stuff so quickly turns into clutter. There's no good place to keep it, and there's no good way to organize it. Do you have stuff like that? Do you wonder what to do with it? The first thing to do is to stop buying it and bringing it home. That's what I've had to do. I remind myself that I don't *have to* have anything. I have all I need.

When I feel the impulse to buy something, I've started asking myself a few questions: "Where am I going to put this? What am I going to do with it? How often will I actually use it?" If we can stop bringing stuff in the door, then it becomes easier to thin out the stuff we have.

One of the reasons I am committed to dealing better with my accumulated stuff is that I have noticed how it clutters not only my home but also my mind; it keeps me from thinking clearly. All the things around me vie for my attention. Maybe it's because of the way I am wired, but my stuff has a way of dancing around and distracting me from what's important. I have all these things that don't really have a place or serve a purpose in my life, so I spend a lot of energy trying to make them fit in. Only recently have I been smart enough to realize that I don't have to keep every little trinket I've ever owned or been given.

At first it seemed wasteful to think of tossing out my doodads, but I have adopted a new perspective: just go ahead and throw them away. I'll never miss them, they're just in the way, and since no one else needs more clutter in their lives, I've decided not to pass off my junk to someone else.

Facing up to my stuff problem is for my benefit. It's going to save me money in the long run, and it's going to clear out my life so I can see things more clearly.

I have a greeting card propped up in my office. It is stark black, scrawled with a line often attributed to the Japanese poet Masahide. It says: "Barn's burnt down. Now I can see the moon!" And how I love to be able to see the things that matter.

How's the view of the moon in your life, Smart Girl?

Life Doesn't Come with Guarantees

Taking our eyes off the stuff of life frees us to consider how much we have to be thankful for—and how easily it could disappear. There was a day not too long ago when a woman moved straight from her father's house to her husband's house, and her financial situation depended entirely on the man in her life. If anything happened to her husband, she often was left a poor widow with meager resources. Unless she was among the few who could go home and live with a father of means, she was left to hold her household together with whatever limited resources she could muster.

When my grandfather on my father's side, John Robert, died from a mining accident, his wife, Mary Jane, was forced to provide for her five children with no outside income. That was in the days before pensions and insurance settlements, and she had no other means of support. So my grandmother used her creativity and turned her home into a boardinghouse. She rented rooms and provided meals and clean linens for people doing business with the mines. Thus, she supported her family for a few years until the second disaster hit: the boardinghouse burned down. Family lore says she was able to save only a pitcher of buttermilk.

And then she started all over again. She had no other option. She moved to another place, and Mary Jane's boardinghouse reopened. Her children were a little older by then and helped out by working, but still the main role of family support was hers.

I'm sure that earlier in her life my grandmother never dreamed she would be the sole support of her children, but when she suddenly found herself a single mom, she turned into a savvy Smart Girl in record time. Hers was not a path any of us would choose, but Smart Girls trust God for provision and prepare themselves for any eventuality. They make it their business to know what's going on with the family finances. Since none of us wants a daddy-husband in other areas, we surely don't expect our husbands to bear all the burden of our finances. Mutual knowledge and supportive discussions about the overall financial picture place husbands and wives on an equal footing, where both can be informed about their money.

What if your husband is one of those men who simply does not want to discuss financial issues? He may have no ulterior motive. He may just assume that it's his role and you shouldn't have to worry about such things. From his perspective, he's taking care of everything and you are safe. In that situation, a Smart Girl at least needs to know where the papers are kept. You may not be able to get your husband to willingly discuss finances, but if you know where the papers are filed, you won't be left high and dry if there is a future problem.

In addition, establishing your own savings now—not someday, but *now*—is the hallmark of a Smart Girl. An emergency fund that earns only a small percentage of interest is better than no emergency fund at all. Even a little money stuck in a jar for a rainy day is better than having to check under the sofa cushions for bread and milk money.

There are no guarantees, and Smart Girls know that. Married women can become single women in an instant, and single women who hoped they would marry may find their dream delayed indefinitely. God is always your protector and provider, no matter what your circumstances. You, however, are responsible to prepare your heart and mind for whatever life role you are called upon to play.

Few things make a woman feel as helpless and hopeless as finding herself in difficult circumstances with no resources. I cannot tell you how many times I have spoken with women who are trapped in marriages without mercy, not allowed to have money or to have control over any of the household funds. They're even more vulnerable to financial disaster than the woman who willingly relies on her husband to handle all the finances. In both cases, they could be left defenseless in case of abandonment, divorce, or death.

I don't want to sound overly harsh or stir up worries, but each of us is responsible to use the brain God gave us. No matter your current marital status, I encourage you to educate yourself about how to make and save money. Read as much as you can about ways to make your money grow.

When one of my wisest Smart Girl friends went through a divorce, she received a small settlement. She used that money to buy a house that was in terrible condition. She then remodeled it, sold it, and bought another house. She had learned how to do this in childhood. Her mother was a remodeler who taught her daughter the do-it-yourself skills of transforming a fixer-upper into a home with curb appeal. Today, my friend earns a livable income by doing what she knows how to do. She works hard, but she is content with her ability to provide for herself.

Other women choose to go back to school, to learn about investments, to renew teaching certificates, or to start cottage industries. Smart Girls keep their eyes and ears open for ways they can be wise about money.

I love that Smart Girl described in Proverbs 31. When King Lemuel's mother told her son what to look for in a woman, she included these attributes:

> She inspects a field and buys it.
> > With money she earned, she plants a vineyard.
> She does her work with energy,
> > and her arms are strong.
> She knows that what she makes is good.
> > Her lamp burns late into the night.
> She makes thread with her hands
> > and weaves her own cloth. (vv. 16–19 NCV)

This mother-in-law-to-be knew that her daughter-in-law needed to be smart about money and how to make it—even if she was marrying her wonderful, faultless son.

One of the most inspiring women I have ever met is Marie Chapian. I credit her with teaching me some of the greatest life lessons about becoming a Big Girl and ultimately a Smart Girl. Her example has been stellar.

Years ago when Dr. Chapian unexpectedly found herself the single mother of two little girls, she was totally unprepared for the job. She couldn't drive, couldn't set her own watch, and was completely overwhelmed with what she had to do to survive. She says she lay around for six months in an emotional pool of self-pity, and then one morning she got out of bed, looked in the mirror, and the words from Jeremiah 31:3 came to her: "Yea, I have loved thee with an everlasting love: therefore with lovingkindness have I drawn thee" (KJV).

That day she began to live. In fact, she not only began to live, she became passionate about life and all that it held for her and her two precious girls. She had no finances, but she did what she could with what she had. She drew on her creativity to make a loving home for her girls. She tells of painting the girls' shoes with house paint because she could not afford to buy them new ones. She made her girls' lives as rich and wonderful as they could be with no money in her pocket for *things*. She learned to drive and to set her own watch, and she even went back to school to get her PhD.

Dr. Chapian raised two incredible girls, became a renowned psychotherapist, travels the world, and has authored or coauthored more than thirty books, including the classic work *Talk Truth*, which has been more recently published as *Telling Yourself the Truth*. If ever there was a Smart Girl who found her purpose in life in spite of abandonment and financial destitution, it is Marie Chapian. She is living proof that it can be done with the strength that only God can provide!

And God will be with you every step of the way too. It may take a lot of imagination at this point in your life to think about being single and relying on the Lord for your very bread as Dr. Chapian did. You may be yearning for the freedom to do your own thing or you may be longing to marry the love of your life. You may be happily married and can never dream that someday you may be your own sole support. No matter their current situations, Smart Girls take the long look down the road of life, realize there are no guarantees, and prepare accordingly.

It All Belongs to God Anyway

I want to close this chapter with a word of exhortation from the apostle Paul. In writing from a Roman prison to thank the church at Philippi for a gift they'd sent to him, he was careful to assure them that, although he was grateful for their care during his imprisonment, he had learned the true secret of being content.

> But I rejoiced in the Lord greatly that now at last your care for me has flourished again; though you surely did care, but you lacked opportunity. Not that I speak in regard to need, for I have learned in whatever state I am, to be content: I know how to be abased, and I know how to abound. Everywhere and in all things I have learned both to be full and to be hungry, both to abound and to suffer need. I can do all things through Christ who strengthens me. (Phil. 4:10–13 NKJV)

Ultimately, everything we have comes from and belongs to God. He is our Source and Resource. Smart Girls know that loving God and trusting Him will always put the lack of money or the abundance of money in proper perspective.

Chapter 5

Is It True? Is It Kind? Is It Necessary?

Smart Girls Think Twice About Words

didn't know they would be the last words we would speak to each other. If I could have chosen what I wanted to say in a moment of parting, I would have chosen these, but I really didn't know.

I was in California speaking at a conference and my mother was in an Alabama hospital. She'd been sick for a few days but was quite content with her situation. She liked her room, she liked her nurses, and she even liked the food. I had no idea that she would leave this world before I could get back and see her again. But she did.

She had been fragile for several years. After she broke a hip and it failed to heal, she was left a virtual invalid. Her world became small, but her capacity to communicate remained large. She checked her e-mail regularly and kept a cell phone near her bed. I always knew it would take about three rings for her to answer. We talked twice a day and, being her only child, I visited in person as often as I could.

When I called her from California that last weekend, she told me she wasn't feeling as well as before. I called several more times to check on her, and with each call I could tell she was feeling worse. As had long been our tradition each time we parted, whether in person or on the phone, I closed every conversation with "I love you," and she always said, "I love you too."

Those were the last words we spoke to one another. She died before I could get to her bedside.

But it was all right in my spirit. I knew we had said everything that needed to be said. We closed that last chapter of our lives together with "I love you," and although I miss her more than I ever knew I would, there are no regrets.

Saying the words you need to say when you need to say them is a worthy goal for every Smart Girl. We never know when a conversation may be our last encounter with someone we love, leaving one of us to hold in our heart either thankfulness or regret for the words spoken or left unsaid.

A Life-or-Death Decision

The Bible has a lot to say on the importance of words. We find one of the strongest statements on this subject in the book of Proverbs: "Death and life are in the power of the tongue" (18:21 NASB). And the book of James gives this enlightening description of what happens when we fail to think twice about our words:

> We all make many mistakes. If people never said anything wrong, they would be perfect and able to control their entire selves, too
> . . . but no one can tame the tongue. It is wild and evil and full of deadly poison. We use our tongues to praise our Lord and

Father, but then we curse people, whom God made like himself. Praises and curses come from the same mouth! My brothers and sisters, this should not happen. Do good and bad water flow from the same spring? My brothers and sisters, can a fig tree make olives, or can a grapevine make figs? No! And a well full of salty water cannot give good water. (3:2, 8–12 NCV)

You and I make an impact on other people by what we say. We can offer them life-infused words or we can throw death darts at them. We can purpose to bless them or we can determine to curse them simply by our choice of words.

My hairstylist, Rodney, has a gracious way of giving words of affirmation to the women who visit his salon. He speaks kind words of encouragement and offers a listening ear to weary women who sit in his chair. He is a focused listener who truly hears his clients' words, and he often writes cards of kindness, sympathy, and support to those who are in pain. When you sit in Rodney's chair, you have his undivided attention; he doesn't get distracted by chatting with other people in the shop. His job is to beautify hair, but he draws on the power of words to beautify hearts and uplift spirits as well.

Compliments breathe amazing life into a woman's soul. When someone says that she loves your outfit, comments that your jewelry is beautiful, or asks "What's that great perfume you're wearing?" she has offered you words of life. You hold your head up a little higher because someone has noticed something special about you. When it happens to me, I appreciate it so much. I have learned that a compliment can have a long shelf life, and I love to help others stock up on their confidence.

On a recent family vacation, my husband, Charlie, and I took our five grandchildren to the continental breakfast in the hotel. We seated them at a table, found out what they wanted, and then began gathering their food. The children quietly talked among themselves while they waited for us to return with their breakfasts.

When I set their food in front of them and turned to go fill a plate for myself, a woman sitting several feet away said, "Are those your grandchildren?" When I said yes, she lavished this grandmother's soul with words of life. "They are so well behaved," she said. "You don't see much of that these days."

I grinned from ear to ear and thanked her profusely. Of course, when I went back to the children, I told them how proud I was to hear those good words about them and thanked them for remembering their manners. As their parents appeared one by one, I told them what had been said and reiterated how proud I was of the job they were doing in raising their children. One comment from a stranger sent words of life washing over the whole Silvious clan that day. That woman never knew how she blessed all of us with that one compliment. In the same way, your words of life can bless others in ways you may never imagine.

> Kind words can warm for three winters, while harsh words can chill even in the heat of summer.
>
> —CHINESE PROVERB

Of course, death can be in our words as well. We all know it, yet we sometimes forget and find ourselves brought up short with a painful reminder.

One day I was chatting with a man as we waited in line to transact some business at the cell phone company. We began talking about words for some reason, which led him to describe a recent incident from his own life. He'd been chatting casually with two women when they started bitterly denouncing the war in Iraq. Having been the commander of a military police unit in Iraq, he didn't enjoy hearing their negative and harsh words on a topic they knew so little about. But he listened and waited, thinking they soon would change the subject and move on. "I had no bone to pick with them," he said. "They were welcome to their opinions." But finally it became obvious they weren't going to stop. He showed me how he then reached down to his knees with both hands and tucked his trouser cuffs into the top of what obviously were prostheses. He had lost both legs in Iraq. He said he looked up at the women but said nothing. He didn't have to. They gulped and fell silent.

Smart Girls think twice before speaking because they know that words of death can boomerang in their faces and cause them to regret ever opening their mouths.

Filter Your Words Carefully

One of the most practical ways to avoid awkward situations in which we find ourselves desperately wishing we could snatch back our words is to first filter them through that familiar old grid of *Is it true? Is it kind? Is it necessary?* A comment that is absolutely true may not be kind or truly necessary.

A fellow speaker of mine had a difficult time at a conference where we both were on the program. She was off the mark and had trouble connecting with the audience. They were restless and didn't get her humor. I really felt for her, and some of the comments I heard in the restroom later were not very complimentary. I heard a few women (those with the gift of mercy) come up to her afterward and generously express their appreciation for what she'd said. She sold a respectable number of her books and received a pat on the back from the pastor. At dinner that night, she said she felt good about the day and that she thought she'd done great. The fact remained, she hadn't.

Yet it wouldn't have done a bit of good at that time for her to be told anything contrary to what she believed. She didn't ask me for a critique, so I applied the grid of *Is it true? Is it kind? Is it necessary?*—and didn't say anything. Sometimes we Smart Girls need to be smart enough to keep our thoughts to ourselves.

I'd learned that lesson the hard way. I blush now to think how wrong I was and how much pain I inflicted on another woman with my unfiltered comments. At one time she and I were involved in many of the same activities, so we had frequent occasion to interact. It seemed to me that she continuously came at me with put-downs and delighted in sarcastic jabs. Patient soul that I am (not!), I soon tired of it and told her so. I self-righteously proceeded to tell her exactly how and why I thought her behavior was wrong and that I wanted her to stop. That's about all I remember of the conversation. I am sure she could tell you every word I stung her with.

> A long dispute means that both parties are wrong.
>
> —VOLTAIRE

I thought I had done the wise thing by getting my feelings out on the table, but I didn't stop for a moment to think about how I had wounded her. Although we still often found ourselves in the same place at the same time, our interactions were strained and neither of us made an effort to reconnect.

Several years later she came to me and asked to talk. We both had grown and been mellowed by the knocks of life since the conversation. She asked me to forgive her for holding bitterness toward me. *Forgive her?* I immediately was convicted about my own heavy-handed reaction and asked her to forgive me. We talked through the stupidity of the situation and forgave one another on the spot. Many times since then I've started to open my mouth to say something and that little reminder—Is it true? Is it kind? Is it necessary?—has popped up on the screen of my mind. It's a great phrase that you might want to jot down on a sticky note and post it where you'll often be reminded to apply it.

Putting a Stop
to Crimes of the Mouth

Smart Girls are careful with their speech because they know that their words reveal their character. Pleasant, respectful words are the root of good manners and reflect the true heart of the person speaking. Civility in our culture has plummeted to a sad level, and the use of unkind, demeaning words is more rampant than ever before. I attribute much of this to a failure on the part of parents to set limits on the sort of language they will accept from their children.

I sometimes hear women complain about their children calling them names and giving them back talk, and I wonder, *Who's in charge at their house?* When we were raising our three sons, we made it clear that they lived in our home as well-loved children, not as the people in charge. If they even thought about talking back to one of us, they quickly discovered that the inmates were not allowed to run the asylum! We invited free and open discussion and they knew we were always available to talk through the things on their hearts, but they also knew that even a hint of disrespect would bring the discussion to a halt. If they wanted to keep on, then discipline started. Some things just are not acceptable, not even a little bit.

If parents don't expect and require appropriate speech, they won't get it. It takes daily training with continual reminders to mold children into respectful, mannerly adults. My friend Heidi has two great kids. From their earliest days of parenting, she and her husband have faithfully insisted that the boys take responsibility for their words. Any time they speak unkindly or fail to respond in a mannerly way (which is rare), she refers to their behavior as a *crime of the mouth*. At each occurrence, she requires them to stop and verbally identify the specific nature of their crime, then go back to whomever they sinned against and make it right.

If you have children at home, I encourage you to keep on keeping on when it comes to teaching them to watch their words carefully. Don't give up. Stay on them about the way they answer adults and saying *please* and *thank you*. If you don't train them, no one else will. But if you do, your hard work will pay off for years to come. Someday they will move into positions of responsibility where their attention to etiquette will give them a true advantage over their peers who didn't cut their teeth at your good manners academy.

Of course, choosing our own words carefully is just as important, maybe more so. It's clear to me that rude adults influence their children to be rude. And each time we fail to filter our words, we add to the general decline in our culture toward using discourteous, cheap, or uncouth words. A Smart Girl can help change that trend by deciding that, whatever happens, she will use only words that are respectful, words that honor others, herself, and the God she serves.

In chapter 2 we looked at God's red flag against taking His name in vain. When we ignore that red flag, we not only show disrespect for our holy God but we also devalue ourselves. Cursing is a habit that shows smallness of heart and spirit, and it has no place in the speech of a Smart Girl who loves her Lord.

Peter, Jesus' friend and disciple, was a weathered fisherman who probably knew how to curse with the worst of them. When this rugged man's man began to follow Jesus, he believed with his whole heart. One day, in answer to Christ's question, "Who do you say that I am?" Peter replied, "You are the Christ, the Son of the living God" (Matt. 16:16 NASB). Peter passionately declared himself to be a disciple of Jesus, and we have no record of him swearing until he was backed into a corner and his old habits came oozing out.

The scene is recorded in Matthew 26. Jesus was arrested and taken to be questioned and sentenced. Peter was worried about his friend. He wanted to be close; he wanted to stay with Jesus all the way. But the pressure was mounting, and the atmosphere was becoming more volatile. Peter's adrenaline had to be running high. He wanted to be bold but he wanted to hide. His troubles deepened when two people recognized him and questioned his relationship to the prisoner. This is where we pick up the story.

> A little later the bystanders came up and said to Peter, "Surely you too are one of them; for even the way you talk gives you away."
>
> Then he began to curse and swear, "I do not know the man!" And immediately a rooster crowed.
>
> And Peter remembered the word which Jesus had said, "Before a rooster crows, you will deny Me three times." And he went out and wept bitterly. (vv. 73–75 NASB)

Peter's dialect gave him away to those who stood nearby. His cursing gave him away to himself. He swore and he cursed and he denied the Lord. In Christ's dark hour, Peter reverted to his old, familiar pattern and acted as if he didn't know Jesus at all.

I think my desire to act as if I do know Jesus is the reason I've become so aware of the words I speak. If I wouldn't say them in the presence of Christ or as an ambassador of Christ, why on earth would I say them in any circumstance, even if I'm irritated and trying to make a point? I don't think there is room in the life of a Smart Girl for carelessly using some of the uncouth words so common in our culture today. Certain vulgar phrases—such as "That pisses me off" or "That really sucks"—are not technically cursing, but they contain crude references that just don't belong in polite company. I honestly think some people who use them don't know what they mean, or maybe they do and they somehow think vulgarity makes them sound hip. Whatever the reason, coarse language makes even the most beautiful lips unappealing.

Just as we remind the little children in our family that "potty talk" is not nice or acceptable, I think Smart Girls are well served in remembering that vulgarity and swearing are not nice or acceptable for adults either. I'll confess that in my younger years I occasionally would say a curse word to make a point, especially when I was angry. But now I'm a Big Girl, and I'm trying to be a Smart Girl. I have chosen to leave cursing and vulgar language out of my vocabulary because I believe it is the right thing to do. No one is forcing me. It's a choice I've made out of respect for myself, for others, and for God.

Choosing Cool Words in the Heat of the Moment

Of course, speaking words of life and honor is not always easy, especially when deeply felt emotions are involved. Words between husbands and wives particularly are a big deal, maybe a much bigger deal than we realize because that relationship is so unique and so vulnerable. Too often, unkind, unfeeling words are tossed around without any thought about how they will affect the relationship. Ugly words wielded in anger are like slashing swords, indiscriminate in their damage. Caught up in anger, frustration, and misunderstanding, many couples lapse into hateful words that are hard to forget and impossible to retract.

My husband, Charlie, and I have been together forty plus years. When we first married, we agreed that there was one sentence we would never speak to one another: "I want a divorce." A few times I could have strangled him—or he me—over a difference of opinion, but we agreed never to speak those words, and we never have.

If you're divorced, you might think, *Well, I'm glad that worked for you. It never could have worked for me.* And I want to say to you, my sister, I understand. Things happen that we never intend, and I get that. It's just that sometimes if you determine ahead of time what you will and will not say in a marriage, you can head off problems. It's no guarantee of marital bliss, but it certainly can help cement your commitment.

It's probably a good thing that Charlie and I decided never to discuss divorce because there have been a few situations that could have taken us to the brink, with me in the driver's seat speeding us along with my fiery, proud words. I remember one particularly silly and unnecessary argument in our early years. I'd been out to a wedding while he stayed home to care for our boys. When I came in, he made the mistake of asking where I had been.

> Better to live on a corner of the roof than share a house with a quarrelsome wife.
>
> —PROVERBS 21:9 NIV

Well, I didn't like his tone. He knew where I had been! I immediately took offense when I should have taken a deep breath and recognized that he just wanted me to come home and help him with the boys. He wanted me to be there.

So before he had a chance to say anything else, I said, "I hate you!" Wasn't that lovely? I can't believe those words came out of my mouth, but they did. Clearly, I don't hate him, and I didn't hate him then, but I felt the need to use words that would hurt. And so, essentially, I challenged him to a fight. But he didn't pick up the gauntlet I had thrown down, and my little display of disrespect and verbal battering fell flat. Not only did Charlie refuse to reciprocate with mean, hateful words of his own, he didn't stay around to discuss my opinions. He left the room, and that was the end of the discussion. Talk about frustrating!

I don't suggest that avoiding a discussion is the way to handle an argument either. If you're the silent type, I encourage you to stay around to talk things through, or at least make an appointment to talk after you both have cooled down. As for Charlie and me, we called a truce on our little battle the next morning, but I still remember how those words came out like bullets.

Over the years, I've learned to say what I mean and mean what I say but also to remember how my words hit the other person's ears. Kind, firm words are easier to accept than fiery, spiteful words crafted to hurt.

Ephesians 4:29–32 offers the best guidelines I know of for choosing words that bring life rather than death to our relationships:

> Do not let any unwholesome talk come out of your mouths, but only what is helpful for building others up according to their needs, that it may benefit those who listen. And do not grieve the Holy Spirit of God, with whom you were sealed for the day of redemption. Get rid of all bitterness, rage and anger, brawling and slander, along with every form of malice. Be kind and compassionate to one another, forgiving each other, just as in Christ God forgave you. (NIV)

Following this advice is easier when we prepare our words ahead of time. You just can't go wrong with thinking before you speak. That's far less painful than speaking out and wishing you had thought a little longer. In other words, Smart Girls choose to respond rather than react.

Reacting is easy; it's just letting the first thing that pops into your head pop right out of your mouth. But the Scriptures say, "Spouting off before listening to the facts is both shameful and foolish" (Prov. 18:13). Response takes a little more time because it requires some thoughtfulness. *How will my words be heard? How will what I say influence the people around me? Am I communicating how I really feel or is this just a knee-jerk reaction? Will I feel the same tomorrow, or am I just angry at the moment?*

The decision of whether to react or respond is one we usually have to make in a split second. Many of the ways we respond can be preplanned as we think through phrases that are positive and offer hope. If we get these in our heads, then we won't jump in with the first thought that rolls off our tongues. The writer of Proverbs admonishes, "Listen to the words of the wise; apply your heart to my instruction. For it is good to keep these sayings in your heart and always ready on your lips" (22:17–18).

Talking to Yourself Can Be a Good Thing

Much of how we tend to react in any given situation is predetermined by our self-talk—what we say to ourselves, what we call ourselves, and what we ask ourselves. Self-talk is that inner voice that reasons with us, argues with us, and sometimes gives us those words we blurt out before thinking them through. What you say to yourself is more important than what others say to you or about you. You have a much louder megaphone on the stage of your life than anyone else who walks through it. You can encourage your heart with the words you speak to yourself, or you can discourage yourself with unkind, uncaring, or even hopeless words.

I talked recently with Diane, a woman who had been maligned by her friend Ellen. Despite the fact that these two had been close for several years, their friendship had fallen apart. Diane was lamenting the fact that Ellen had said so many unkind things about her. "She told everyone that I lied about her and used her. I never did any such thing! If anything, that's what she's doing to me. I can't believe it! I'll never get over this. She has ruined my life!"

At this point, Diane began to cry. I sat with her and let her cry for a few minutes, then we began to talk. "Honey, I know this hurts and hurts deeply. You feel betrayed. Ellen has been your good friend, but now she has turned her back on you. That's all true. We don't know why, and we may never know, but I have to remind you that

Ellen can only hurt you as much as you give her the power to hurt you. Remember all those 'self-talk' conversations we've had? Now is the time to get a grip and think about what you are telling yourself."

As we talked, Diane was still hurting, but she began to realize that she could either let the situation make a dent in her soul by absorbing and lingering over all the things Ellen had said or she could speak the truth to herself like this: *I am sorry that Ellen feels the way she does. I never want to lose a friend, but this is her call. She has chosen her words, and she has chosen to walk away from me. I've tried to talk with her, and she has given me the cold shoulder. That really gets my goat, but I am going to speak good words to myself, and while I'm at it, I am going to tell God all about this. This hurts deeply, but I don't have to keep letting it consume my thoughts. I'm just going to give the whole mess to Him. That surely does feel better than stewing over what Ellen said.* Now, Diane was not instantly healed from the pain of Ellen's betrayal, but she had made a good start. She was no longer stuck telling herself how awful and unfair it was that her friend had turned on her. Such experiences take time to process, but getting her self-talk under control was essential to her ability to move forward.

Here's the truth for Diane and you and me: we can't control the things that happen to us, but we surely can determine how we will speak to ourselves, and to others, about those things. When a similar situation happened to me, I found that telling one good friend who could remain unbiased and just listen helped me a lot. When I had said how I felt several times and then heard myself beginning to describe the circumstances again, I realized I was tired of talking about it and tired of thinking about it. I quit blaming the person who hurt me, I quit blaming myself, I chose to give up my right to punish her verbally or even in my thoughts, and I moved on. Taking charge of our self-talk makes it so much easier to adjust our outlook on a difficult situation.

Smart Girls learn the art of talking to others and to themselves in kind, helpful ways. Proverbs 10:32 says, "The lips of the righteous know what is fitting" (NIV). The writer of Proverbs also notes that "too much talk leads to sin" (10:19). A time of silence often can help us hear what God wants us to say. I've noticed that when I shut my mouth and quiet my mind, God invariably speaks truth to my soul. He prepares me to respond rather than react. His wisdom is unlike that of any other, and the words that He actually puts in our mouths are precious.

> The longer I live the more convinced I become that life is 10 percent what happens to us and 90 percent how we respond to it.[1]
>
> —CHARLES R. SWINDOLL

Our words are what we use to communicate from the inside out. They tell volumes about the health of our thoughts because we only can verbalize what has passed through our brains. A dear friend of mine called this week and said, "I think I've been whining, and I don't believe I want to keep that up." I listened as she listed all of the bounty in her life for which she is grateful, and then she said, "But I think I've gotten in a habit of complaining about what I have to do, and I've realized I wouldn't have it any other way. There are women all over the world who would love to have the life that I live." I smiled at these words from one of my Smart Girl friends who had forgotten to be smart for a short while and then realized she didn't like it. She remembered that the words we speak influence the quality of the life we live. She, like you and like me, has been richly blessed, and she doesn't want to lose sight of that fact.

The ability to speak gives us astounding power in our own lives and in the lives of others. With that power comes great responsibility. Let's remember that what we say is heard not only by others, which is significant enough, but also is heard by the God who loves us and who has given us all that we have. How can we hurt His heart with careless, ungrateful words? May the prayer of our lives be: "Let the words of my mouth and the meditation of my heart be acceptable in Your sight, O LORD, my strength and my Redeemer" (Ps. 19:14 NKJV).

Chapter 6

Relatively Speaking

Smart Girls Think Twice About Family

The baby girl in the older man's arms seems content as she holds her toy in her hands and looks at the camera. The man, dressed in a white shirt and dress pants, is slightly stooped as he holds the baby with the casual grasp of a longtime father. The baby is me. The man is my grandfather Charles Mitchell. And the picture is in the Mitchell Family Cookbook, which contains old family recipes interspersed with family photos and vignettes from the lives of those who have gone before us.

Opposite the only picture I've ever seen of my grandfather and me is a remembrance written by one of his daughters, my Aunt Marie.

My Daddy

He was always kind to us and did many things that a lot of fathers wouldn't do, such as play games and make us treats. He could draw, paint a picture, and I remember Mama asking him to make the dinner table longer, which he did several times as our family increased. A funny thing about him when we were young was that he never cursed, but if he hit his finger while hammering he would say, "Aw, rats!" That was as close to a curse word as he ever said, and we kids would run and tell Mama that Daddy had cursed.

He was the fire chief in town and was compassionate to the people whose houses burned down. He often lobbied help for them when they were destitute.

When Mama died at the age of thirty-six, he was never the same. The fire chief's job was taken from him by a friend, and he had a hard time making a living for all of us after that. He painted signs but his heart was never there. He would often leave them until he needed the money desperately. This much I know. He loved us.

My grandfather died when I was two, so his children's memories and a picture of me in his arms are all I have of him. My parents, too, are gone now, and although I am an only child, I have aunts, uncles, and cousins who have been part of my life since before my earliest memory. All of these family members are part of a history that continues to be written in my life book. Their impact on me makes up a foundational portion of who I am.

For me, as for most people, the connection with family is tender. So much of who we are emanates from the relatives who have gone before us and who surround us in our family. No matter if you see family as agreeably pleasant or obnoxiously troublesome, they are part of who you are. We all grow up with their history and DNA running through us.

What threads of history and wisps of memory tie together the sum of your knowledge of family? Maybe you long to know more, or maybe you wish you knew a little less. Sometimes family relationships can be the hardest of all. The closeness, the blood ties, and the shared history can make for interesting and occasionally difficult interactions, but a Smart Girl carefully considers family and all that it means to her.

In Touch with the Past

A lot of family ways are passed along, generation to generation. How many times have you and I said, "I will never be like my mother"? Guess what. We *are* like our mothers. And our grandmothers and our great-grandmothers. Knowingly or not, we have inherited their mannerisms, their familiar phrases, and sometimes even their *favorite bad feelings*.

My friend Lynda Elliott, a life coach, introduced me to this phrase several years ago. She explained that a favorite bad feeling is the comfortable place to which we revert when things don't go our way. Some people yell. Some people release a torrent of words and then fall silent for a while. Some just clam up until they decide to speak again. Other people slam doors, clean house, drive fast, or seek out the nearest stash of chocolate. Whatever your favorite way of dealing with frustration, it probably can be traced to something one of your parents or one of your close family members did when you were a child, and so it is as natural to you as breathing.

I have two great daughters-in-law who are a delight to my soul. After raising three sons, to have daughters has been amazing. We girls often laugh among ourselves about our favorite bad feelings.

One mild spring day the three of us were standing around my

van, making plans to go to lunch together, while my grandchildren played inside the vehicle. When we'd finalized our choice of restaurant, my daughter-in-law Heather opened the door to the van and *Boom!* her daughter Rachel fell out. Unbeknownst to her mother, she'd been leaning against the door. The sound of her impact on the driveway was horrific. Shocked and worried, each of us women immediately went to our favorite bad feelings.

First, Heather began to cry. You're probably thinking, *Well, of course she cried; her daughter had just fallen out of the van.* But in fact, crying is Heather's immediate response to any event or situation that troubles her heart. Crying is just what she does.

Then I did what I usually do when upset. I got angry and made rules. Pointing at nothing in particular (I use my instructional pointer finger freely at moments like this), I proclaimed, "From now on, no one rides in this van without being strapped in!" Never mind that the motor was not running, there was no driver, and we weren't yet going anywhere! Somehow making rules seems to help me feel more in control when a crisis strikes. So there I stood, pointer finger extended.

At that moment my other daughter-in-law, Sandi, piped in from the well of her favorite bad feeling. When things go wrong, her immediate response is to try to make everyone happy. She wants peace, and she wants to make sure that everyone is okay with whatever is going on. So while Heather cried and I made a rule, Sandi said, "Gan Gan, I think she knows that rule!"

Well, that brought us back to reality. I dropped my finger, and we all rushed to check on Rachel. I'm glad to report she was fine—only a little black eye—but we learned a lot that day about the women in our family and our favorite bad feelings.

You may not recognize your own favorite bad feeling, but if you think twice about how you usually react in stressful situations, you probably will identify it. And if you can identify it, the next step is to assess whether your typical response is helpful to your life today or needs to be discarded.

Many of our favorite bad feelings are carryovers from childhood, coping mechanisms that worked then but might not be appropriate for us as adults. As a child, my primary coping mechanism was to cry. I learned the tears from my mother because when I was very young, crying was her favorite bad feeling. By the time I became a teenager, she had replaced her tears with healthier coping mechanisms. I, however, was finding them quite a satisfying solution. Crying seemed to relieve the stress of whatever was bothering me, and then I could dry my eyes and go on. I did most of my crying in the bed with my dachshund, Emily, curled up in the crook of my legs. I would cry, tell her all about what was wrong, and eventually go to sleep. Tears were accepted in my family, and no one was particularly disturbed when I cried. It was just what I did.

> Family faces are magic mirrors. Looking at people who belong to us, we see the past, present and future.[1]
>
> —GAIL LUMET BUCKLEY

Then I got married. I never thought about how my tears would affect my husband. I expected him to understand that, when I cried, I was dealing with a bad feeling and he needed to listen to me. So although we were happy to be married and loved life on our own, every now and then something would upset me and I would cry. After a few of these episodes, Charlie came to me and said, "I have a hard time with your tears. They don't help." I was astonished. I didn't expect him to do anything about them. They were just my way of expressing a bad feeling. To him, however, they signaled terrible distress, and they left him feeling helpless.

I thought, *Well, if he doesn't like the tears, I'll stop them.* My crying wasn't accomplishing anything and it bothered him, so I needed to find another way to express my bad feelings. I didn't exactly think it through in that order, but I imagine that's where my rule-making came in. I learned that if I make a rule, then I feel as if the situation, whatever it might be, is under control. Now, like every favorite bad feeling, rule-making can create its own problems. That fearsome little statement "If Mama ain't happy, ain't nobody happy" probably originated with some family who had either a crier or a rule maker in the house! The point is, we need to take a second look at coping mechanisms, emotional responses, and other behaviors we've picked up from our family and brought into the present to see how they're working. If your standard reactions tend to create distance, confusion, or condemnation in a situation, maybe it's time to develop a new favorite response.

Is It Time to Break with Tradition?

We tend to carry with us into adulthood not only our own habits of response but also certain expectations of how families traditionally relate to one another—and many times these expectations are rooted in negative past experiences.

I chatted recently with a young friend who said, "My mother isn't speaking to me again."

"Again? Does she stop speaking often?" I asked.

"Oh yes, she got it from Grandmother. I remember when I was a kid Mother would fume about Grandmother not speaking to her. This would go on for weeks. Now that I'm an adult, she does the same thing to me." She laughed it off and said, "I guess when she decides to break her silence, we'll be in touch again. I love her, and I know she loves me. That's just the way she is, but it sure does make it hard at holidays."

I'll bet it does. How can you get together as a family when one member isn't speaking to another member? That's just way too stressful. And yet for many people such conflict is as much a family tradition as tree trimming, carol singing, and cookie baking. Although most of us look forward to times when our lives intersect with our extended family, often the holidays are just a wreck looking for a place to happen.

Family-of-origin beliefs affect our view of the holidays and other special occasions in our lives. Some women fanatically insist that the entire clan gather together for certain holidays or celebrations. They pour themselves into making sure that everyone will come and every detail is perfect. Yet very few families can successfully pull off a Norman Rockwell Thanksgiving or a Hallmark Christmas without some incident that diminishes the glow. Expectations are dashed, feelings get hurt, and it seems the long-anticipated family gathering can't possibly end soon enough. That's really sad because family is such a unique group of people.

Rather than doggedly clinging to tradition, Smart Girls think twice and determine to be flexible in finding a plan that works for everyone or adjusts to changing realities. Doing the same things the same way year after year has pitfalls you may never dream of. What if you have to change it one year? What if circumstances prevent your doing what you always have done?

I well remember when it hit me that clinging to a family tradition could bring sadness instead of comfort. Our first baby, David, and I were living with my parents while Charlie was in Vietnam. Usually we had a great Christmas with a tree, presents, a wonderful meal, and family gathered around. This year my dad was in the bed with a terrible flu, my young husband was fighting a war halfway around the world, and Mother and I were left to "do Christmas" with one-year-old baby David. I remember dressing in the kimono my husband had sent from Vietnam, standing beside the flowers he had ordered for my December 23 birthday, and taking pictures of myself so he could see how happy we were at Christmas. In reality it was pretty bleak.

That's when I realized that holidays are not about observing one particular day or having all the family together. They're about being grateful that we have a family even if we're separated.

And sometimes separation can even be a good thing in family. So often there is a huge effort to bring everyone together because we have an unrealistic picture of what it looks like to be "one big happy family." But like oil and water, some family members just don't mix. A Smart Girl is willing to rethink her view of what will work and try things a different way, especially when it involves trying to meld her family of origin with the family she married into or a family divided by divorce. Good times, relaxed interactions, and stress-free memories are easier to come by when we let go of "but we've always done it this way."

Taking the "I" Out of *Family* Makes Life Incomplete

Closeness with family often ebbs and flows as your own life story develops, but the people in that original unit influenced your early understanding of relationships and they will never be unimportant. Though it may become damaged or frayed, the family bond is never fully destroyed, but each of us plays a part in determining how viable it is. Family is where you start out and, as Robert Frost wrote of home, it's where "they have to take you in."[2] Family is a gift from God that we sometimes overlook until it's too late. Other times family is used and abused until it is too dysfunctional to be of any value. It can get lost in the shuffle of our *becoming*, and it often is derided because of its irritations. Family can be relegated to a pile of excuses: "It's too much trouble" or "They're too far away" or "We have nothing in common anymore."

A Smart Girl, however, will Stop, Look, Listen, and Look Again at the lifelong connections of family, at the relationships that deserve to be nurtured, and even at the value she herself brings to the family. If married, she acknowledges that his family is really her family too. She chooses to value them as she does her own, a decision for which she will never be sorry. And when it comes to the family she has helped to create—those exasperating people who demand Cheerios for breakfast, who often make messes at the wrong time, and whose actions occasionally grate on her soul—she cherishes each one as part of that astonishingly wonderful organism called family.

> Call it a clan, call it a network, call it a tribe, call it a family. Whatever you call it, whoever you are, you need one.[3]
>
> —JANE HOWARD

A Smart Girl thinks twice before she comes to the conclusion that *I* is greater than *we*. Being part of a family means being a piece of the pie but not the whole pie. It means being one segment of the orange or one egg in the carton or one crayon in the box. The singular part, while separate, can't be removed from the whole without leaving both the whole and the part incomplete.

A sweet friend of mine lost two of her four children. After they died, she never again wanted to have a family picture made. "They're not all here," she would say. Her family group was missing two pieces, and there was no way to close the gap. That family's *we* had been diminished, and the ache in her heart was great. It is impossible to lose a part of the whole without being affected. The family unit just doesn't look the same anymore. Everyone eventually will adjust to a new normal, but the loss of a member means the family is forever changed.

When you are part of a family, you know that your presence and your participation matter to the whole. Younger Smart Girls probably need more of a wake-up call in this area. When you're young, it feels as if family will always be there, and once you're out of the fold, it can seem confining to rejoin the group, even for a few days. I understand, but trust me on this: you will never regret thinking *we* instead of *I* when it comes to family. Focusing solely on *I* means choosing independence and isolation. Choosing to emphasize *we* brings community and connection, the comfort of building a shared history.

I remember when I was seventeen and very focused on *I*—a time when I wanted family and yet didn't want family. I was working at a camp in North Carolina and had to have an emergency appendectomy. I felt alone, but I didn't want my parents to worry about me or to make the ten-hour trip from Washington DC to see me. They knew I was going into surgery, and one of my friends would call them when it was over. That, to my mind, should have satisfied them. I was not surprised, however, when a nurse came into the room several hours after the surgery to tell me I had visitors. I was alert enough to know it was the middle of the night because everything was dark, but I wasn't prepared for my mixed reaction when my parents walked into the room. They had started out when they heard the news and had driven through the wee hours of the morning, then wrangled their way into the hospital to see their child. Their view of the situation was that they wanted to see for themselves that I was fine. My view was, "I can handle this. I have my friends." I was glad to see them but felt frustrated, believing they didn't think I could deal with life apart from them. I was very *I* focused. Of course, now that I'm a parent, I know that if one of my children was having surgery in a far place, I would gladly drive all night to be with them. That's what families do. The transition from *I* to *we* has taken place, and I have great passion for the whole.

Are you in a place of *I* or *we*? That may be a point to ponder in some of your Smart Girl therapy moments.

Now let me add a small caveat at this point: not every family wants to be a group of *we*. Some family members have chosen their own way and will rebuff any effort on your part to be involved in their lives. If that's the case, then you don't have to keep making monumental efforts to be a *we-some*. You can use the Drawbridge Principle. I have taught this principle for years in the context of difficult relationships and have never known it to fail. Here it is: Think of yourself as being in a castle. Now remember that every self-respecting castle is encircled by a moat, and across every moat extends a drawbridge. When your difficult person approaches, you can simply pull up your drawbridge to protect your emotions. You continue to be kind, but you don't invite interaction. You carry on light conversation, but you don't allow the discussion to go deep enough for the other person to inflict damage. You are a Smart Girl who understands the importance of not allowing into your castle anyone—family, friend, or foe—who would be careless with or even damage your emotions.

The Scriptures say, "The name of the LORD is a strong tower; the righteous run to it and are safe" (Prov. 18:10 NKJV). This applies to you, if you are a Christian. You can run into Christ, your refuge and strong tower, and find comfort and safety there. You don't have to make a big to-do about being in your castle. Just go there and pull up your drawbridge, recognizing that once people prove themselves to be toxic, you can relate to them as those who could have been family but have chosen instead to be relatives. There is a difference. Family is a safe, connected group that leaves you emotionally intact and even enhances your life. Relatives are those to whom you are linked by history, but you do not share with them a sense of community and connection. Your job is to be gracious, but you don't have to keep trying to make something happen that neither of you wants.

Coming to Terms with Reality

Families, even the bad ones, are important because they help shape who we become. I hate to even speak of the subject of abuse in the context of family, but unfortunately that is where mental and physical abuse usually occurs. Although it might feel easier just to discount family in the wake of abuse, no matter how you try, you can't truly shake them off or ignore the effects of their behavior. It has made an indelible impression on your life. Understanding your family-of-origin dynamics is key to understanding yourself. Smart Girls know this, and although they may have to draw wide boundaries in order to get along, they don't discount their family's influence on who they have become.

Most of us have a longing in our hearts to believe that our families are *safe*. It is my belief that we all want to be proud of our family members, and if we were to introduce them to our friends, we would want to be able to affirm that they are safe—and probably *sane* would be helpful too. This is true of both the family we come from and the family we've gathered around ourselves in adulthood through marriage and parenting. In some ways, believing your family is safe and sane means you don't have to work so hard at proving that you are safe and sane. Being part of a *good family* says to the world, and to you, that you probably are a good person too. It may be unfair, but a person's family identification establishes her credentials, one way or the other. Sometimes it can be a little schizophrenic because families tend to be a mixed bag with both bad *hombres* and good folks. But for better or worse, they are your family. You have to take them as they are and make the most of it.

Part of making the most of any family situation, whether good or bad, is coming to the realization that God knows, God cares, and for some reason you may not comprehend on this earth, He saw fit to place you in your particular family—both the family you grew up with and the family that gathers around you as you move through your adult years.

> Too many people miss the silver lining because they're expecting gold.[4]
>
> —MAURICE SEITTER

We tend to enter adulthood with great expectations. Young girls do a lot of dreaming about what their lives will be when they grow up: how many children they will have, what their names will be, what their homes will be like, and how Prince Charming will behave after the wedding. Of course, dreams and reality don't always run on parallel tracks. When the two begin to diverge, Smart Girls choose to accept their circumstances. We can dream and dream, yet in the end we'll have to deal with the reality of what is, rather than what could have been.

One of the best lessons I have learned in my journey to becoming a Smart Girl is this: what might have been does not exist, so don't even go there! It saves so much torment and expended energy when we refuse to ponder the *if onlys* and stick to reality. Just because life turns out differently than we expected, that doesn't mean it isn't good. It's just different. But if we remain set on our dreams, we'll miss God's delights. Remember, today is all we are promised. Yesterday is gone, and tomorrow is not yet here, so the Smart Girl accepts God's invitation to live in the moment.

I wonder how different your family life is today from what you wanted it to be. Are you making the best of relating to the child you expected to be cuddly and compliant but who has turned out to be difficult and defiant? Are you holding the household together while your husband travels constantly and you both endure the lonely nights? Are you living single in a family of married brothers and sisters and their children while your heart longs for a mate?

Are you caring for a parent with Alzheimer's who has forgotten who you are? Are you dealing with debilitating illness yourself? These are just slices of the unexpected situations that can challenge our dreams and expectations of life. Much as we may wish our situations were different, we have what we have, and a wonderful serenity comes in accepting each person and each situation as God's plan for us. Amy Carmichael, missionary to India for fifty years, said it best: "In acceptance lies peace."

You can kick against your family situation and moan and groan to the Lord and everyone else. Or you can gently sink into the will of God, recognizing that your family, right now, the way they are, is your assignment for this day. Doing so can calm your heart and give you eyes to see beyond your feelings and fears. When you choose to accept the people in your family as they are, you will find it much easier to cope gracefully with the things they do or say.

Learning to accept the choices of adult children can be one of a mother's greatest challenges. They want to be accepted for who they are, not for who we want them to be, but sometimes it's so hard to let go of our own hopes for them.

When her adult daughter started becoming serious about a young man who just didn't measure up to Jill's dreams for her, life in their household became very tense. Jill made no bones about her feelings toward Sara's boyfriend. The problem was, Sara loved him and wanted to marry him. Jill loudly declared to her friends, "I don't say anything around Sara that would make her think I don't like him," but her attitude sent an unmistakable message: "The man you have chosen to marry is unacceptable." Sara married him anyway, and today Jill freely admits, "I was wrong. He loves my daughter, and I love him." Jill had to humble herself and acknowledge that she didn't necessarily know what was best for Sara, and Sara and her husband had to humble themselves to forgive Jill. They all have reconciled their past disagreements and love being a family.

No matter what choices our children make, we remain their parents. Even when we're certain they need to do something about their health or their attitudes or their spiritual lives or dating lives, we need to realize that people change only because they want to, not because of our pleading or nagging. We can't change who they are and we can't take control of their life choices, but we can let them know that we always will love them.

Best-selling author Barbara Johnson once told me of her own experience in learning this lesson. When she discovered that her son had walked away from all he'd been taught and entered a homosexual lifestyle, she said she was so agitated her teeth itched. She often shared her story openly in public, reaching the point where she realized she could do only two things: love him and pray for him. After that, she knew she had done all she could. She left it up to the Lord to change him.

That's the best choice a Smart Girl can embrace, no matter what her adult child or beloved family member has gotten into. You can love him, pray for him, and let the Lord change him. That's what you can do today and tomorrow and the day after. Such a choice frees you to sincerely offer unconditional love to your family member. You aren't arguing; you're praying. You aren't playing God; you're relying on Him. The only power you have is your love and your prayers.

Growing Your Own Family

The role of family doesn't have to be filled by blood relatives; any group of people wading through life together can serve as your companions through joy, sorrow, and all the in-between times. Having a great group of friends is one of the best gifts you can give yourself.

I have several different groups of friends who make my life richer because of the different ways we have encountered one another. Some of us have come together through our church affiliation, some through mutual ministry, and I even have a group of friends living in different parts of the country who meet for a 7:00 a.m. call every two weeks. We talk about the books we're reading, study the Bible together, and pray for our country and each member of our group. We are bonded uniquely because of our mutual commitment to encouraging one another and expanding our worlds.

Whether single or married, I recommend that you get yourself some girlfriends and discover the beauty of a family of friends. Groups of friends, rather than one-on-one relationships, are generally preferable because the intensity of staying together all the time can leave you feeling as if you have no room to breathe and little room to grow. It is easy to become overly connected and thus limit your opportunities to deepen your relationships with other people. The reality is that best friends at twenty may not qualify at forty. Remember, there is a season to everything, including, in some cases, friendship. Closeness often comes through circumstances, and when those circumstances change, so does the friendship. It doesn't mean that it has ceased to be, but rather it has a different position.

I stopped having a *best friend* many years ago because it occurred to me one day, *If asked, would I know who my second-best or third-best friend is? And does my best friend become my ex-best friend when times and seasons change? Or maybe she'll drop in the ranking from best to fourth best?* Do you see how that can be as sticky as a Venus flytrap?

The family issue can be challenging for a single woman who has not, for whatever reason, gathered a family of husband and children around her. Therefore, the single woman with several close friends who are mutually devoted to one another and who are there for the long haul is rich indeed. She has discovered the blessings of a family dressed up in friends' clothing. Throughout my lifetime, I've had the privilege of knowing many single women who have walked through life for thirty or forty years beside other wonderful friends. Mary Graham, Ney Bailey, Luci Swindoll, Marilyn Meberg, and Pat Wenger are just such a group. You'll recognize some of those names as the Porch Pals at Women of Faith conferences. These mutually caring and supportive women form a small community within a community; they are family. They all are single or single again, and they have lives that are rewarding and full. They travel all over the world together, make their homes close to one another, and share a vibrant faith and profound mutual respect. And they each individually have other friends who weave an even richer texture into their lives.

> Some people are your relatives but others are your ancestors, and you choose the ones you want to have as ancestors. You create yourself out of those values.[5]
>
> —RALPH ELLISON

Of course, the single Smart Girl has her family of origin with whom to relate as well. If they will accept her as single and satisfied, then a good deal of the angst that families experience over single members can be avoided. Not everyone wants to be married, is going to be married, or ultimately stays married, for whatever reason. So the single Smart Girls who live well and show that they are quite content can gain their families' acceptance and blessings.

What Will Your Legacy Be?

Smart Girls understand that legacy is a vital aspect of family connections. What we pass on to future generations is our gift of life or death. Have you simply absorbed what has been handed down to you from your family experience, or have you examined your family's pattern of thinking and decided whether or not it's worth hanging onto? Once you become an adult, you have the option to examine the family "truth" as you have understood it and either embrace or discard it.

A little self-examination for Smart Girls would include questions such as:

- Where does my family stand politically?
- Is my family racist?
- What value do the men in my family place on women?
- What value do the women in my family place on men?
- Does my family have a critical spirit?
- What is my family's attitude toward money?
- Does my family think it is noble to act as if we are poor?
- Is my family generally optimistic or pessimistic?
- Is my family affectionate?
- Does my family exhibit addictive behaviors?
- Does my family practice preventative healthcare?
- What does my family think about God?
- What legacy has my family left to me?

And here's the most important question:

- What do I want to pass on to my family?

If you will take some time to honestly answer these questions, you will see more clearly where you stand in relationship to how your family thinks. You also can decide what you want to pass down from the heritage left to you and what you want to set aside. Smart Girls know that the legacy they leave will give their children and grandchildren either wings to fly or weights around their feet.

They think twice about their relationship to God and how they communicate that to their children. Do your children (no matter what their age) know that their mother loves the Lord? Have they seen evidence that you honor Him, respect Him, talk to Him, and rely on Him for all that you are?

Smart Girls find ways to make sure they leave something of value. We leave a lot in attitude and character and memories, but something tangible your family can remember as being yours will provide a point of reference for their remembering. Bibles with your markings, thoughts, prayers, and notes are priceless treasures. I plan to leave five Bibles with those kinds of notations. I want each of my five grandchildren to know that their grandmother knew the Lord and took notes on what He said! I want them to think twice about what they do and who they are because they remember that their Gan Gan prayed for them and believed in God's plans for them. That is part of the legacy I want to pass on.

Do you have a planned legacy for your children or grandchildren? Some small trinket that often catches their eye at your house can be a lifelong memory maker if you will save it for them. My seven-year-old granddaughter Rachel has had her eye on a starfish paper weight on my desk since she was about three. She has held it in her little girl hands with wonder and asked if she could have it when she got married. I assured her that she could, and now I keep it in a special place where she can hold and admire it but where it is safely preserved for when she gets married. It is valueless in terms of money, but it's a treasure in her brown eyes. So it is saved to be a little reminder someday that her Gan Gan loved her very much. It's all about memories and legacy.

It's all about family.

Chapter 7

You've Gotta Love 'Em

Smart Girls Think Twice About Men

en are different. Not broken, just different. It's hard for our feminine minds to grasp how men can be part of the same species yet be so vastly unlike us.

We're stymied by the way they think and often find ourselves shaking our heads at the things they do. For instance, aren't you amazed at the men who park their carts sideways in the grocery-store aisle while they study the list their wives sent with them? They are totally unaware that they're blocking the aisle as they hunt for their assigned can of peas. Their focus is on getting the job done rather than fitting in with traffic in the grocery-store culture. Or maybe you've seen this one: men who back into parking spaces. They pull forward, blocking traffic, so they can back their vehicle into the space. There seems to be an unwritten law among men that it's okay to stop traffic in order to back into the space so *he* won't be held up by traffic when it's time to leave. That's a "go figure" in my book!

We like men most days, but sometimes we're convinced they'll drive us crazy—and they surely feel the same about us. We appreciate their strength when we need it, but we are quick to push back if we think they are trying to dominate us. We want them to take care of the things that are too hard for us, but they dare not utter a word about our weakness of mind or body. We have no tolerance for the man who has a chauvinistic, "I'm better than you" attitude, but few things turn us off as quickly as the male who hangs back and fails to assert himself at the proper time. Each gender is an enigma to the other.

Don't Expect Him to Think, Feel, or Talk Like You

Learning to accept the distinct "otherness" of the male of the species is a great starting point for improving our relationships with the men in our lives—at home, at work, at church, or at the car-repair shop.

Feminists who have tried to disprove the differences between men and women have found their efforts futile. They can rant and rave, march and cajole, but they can't change the fact that males and females are just plain different on every level. Every mother, like it or not, knows this to be true. While social scientists have tried to explain away the differences between boys and girls as social conditioning, it remains a challenge to interest girls in trucks or boys in dolls. The great majority of males fall into the dump trucks, dirt, and motors camp while the females gravitate toward glitter, games, and dolls. Of course, there are exceptions, but for the majority, the orientation is distinct and unchangeable. It's all a matter of the brain.

Increasing volumes of knowledge are being discovered in the area of brain science, and the distinct differences between male and female brain structure has been one of the premier findings of the past ten years. Researchers have learned that different hormones connect up with the distinctively structured female and male brains, and, as a result, men and women have divergent thought processes and behaviors.[1] In short, we are not alike because our brains are different; each sex was designed by our Creator to be unique.

> When men and women agree, it is only in their conclusions; their reasons are always different.[2]
>
> —GEORGE SANTAYANA

I only wish I had known this early in my marriage. I agonized for years about my husband's supposed emotional deficits. Why did he not feel the way I did? Why did he not want to talk everything through until it was totally solved, sealed, and delivered? Why did he seem to be emotionally "out to lunch" at times? Now I know. It was *his brain*. I'm finally becoming a Smart Girl and have given up the notion that he should respond to me with a woman's emotions. He's a man.

The fact that men are different is cause enough for Smart Girls to think twice about their interactions with the male species. We need to accept the way men are wired and respond accordingly.

It occurred to me years ago that men are like adding machines in the way they process information. They deal with facts one at time, just as they might add a long column of numbers, ultimately arriving at an accurate answer. Women, on the other hand, tend to process the same information like a computer. We may not bother to do the actual math, but we can pull random thoughts from different parts of our brains and almost immediately come up with an answer that's good enough, and probably fairly close to what our male counterpart would deduce. It's just the opposite with the emotional differences between the two sexes. Usually, women want to analyze each detail and word one by one while men are satisfied with drawing some general conclusions and moving on with their lives. Men have to work hard to find and identify what they are feeling, and they rarely feel compelled to talk about it once they do. Women, on the other hand, have lots of feelings and are usually more than happy to discuss them, even if they are subject to change—within the hour.

Have you ever been in a discussion with a man and asked, "But what do you really mean?" Of course, you know he's going to say, "I mean exactly what I said!" but something inside compels us to ask anyway. We women tend to be faster on the draw when it comes to verbalizing our thoughts and emotions, so to question what a man is "really" saying isn't fair. In most cases we need to take a man's words at face value and respond to what he says, not to what we think he is saying. Of course, Smart Girls also wait and watch his behavior, knowing that conversations about feelings he doesn't have or can't acknowledge are meaningless.

A Healthy View of Men Leads to Healthy Relationships

If you think men are buffoons or if you find them frightening or if you think they're what makes life worth living, then your view of men is out of kilter. You need to look in the mirror and ask yourself, "Why do I think men are pigs?" or "Why am I afraid of men?" or "Why do I think I have to have a man or I'll just die?" Your answer to that question will have very little to do with men and everything to do with your view of yourself. For some reason, your experience with men has left you believing they have some incredible control over your life, and therefore, you view yourself as "less than" because of it.

Smart Girls don't make sweeping assumptions about men and react to all males in the same way. They measure each individual by the way he behaves, not by past experiences with other men. Lumping all men into one category is as inaccurate and foolish as assuming that all women are poor drivers. Yes, as we have seen, men generally share some common characteristics because of the way God created them, but each one puts those traits to work in different ways and deserves to be related to as a unique and separate individual whose qualities are measured by his own behavior.

How does he behave most of the time? What can you expect from him? Over a period of time, have you found surprises that trouble you? Or is he consistent in his behavior? How high are his highs and how low his lows? How does he treat other people? How does he treat his mother? How does he treat waitresses and store clerks? What does he do when frustrated by traffic? What kind of language does he use to express himself when under pressure? All of these markers point to the behavior by which you can judge a man.

Your attitude toward men permeates who you are, so much so that your sons and daughters will be profoundly affected by your views. If you're afraid of men or think they all are after only one thing, then your daughter will pick up on that. In possibly subtle yet very real ways your perspective will guide her thinking as she interacts with men. She always will be slightly on guard and will find it hard to trust even the good guys in her life. And your son won't know what to think. He may learn to fear his own maleness because his mother is afraid of men, or he may position himself as an alpha male who women fear because that is all he knows of manhood. No good result will come from a fearful mindset toward men.

By contrast, if you are overly indulgent toward men, excusing bad behavior with a "boys will be boys" attitude or allowing them to mistreat you, you set your children up for a hard fall. If you fail to set clear guidelines for acceptable male behavior, then your son will believe that, as a guy, he has a license to do whatever he wants, and your daughter won't know how to draw boundaries to protect herself in dangerous situations.

If you struggle with your view of men, I encourage you to seek counsel from someone you can trust. Our feelings don't come out of the blue, and it's always to our advantage to at least recognize why we feel as we do. The good news is that none of us has to stay stuck in our views of men. We can challenge our thinking, face our wrong conceptions, and choose to turn them around. In doing so we'll develop better relationships with men by appreciating them for who they are—neither angels nor animals but unique and intriguing creations of God.

Working with Your Differences

Within the work environment, the differences between men and women show up in everything from sales approach to conflict resolution, and Smart Girls figure out how to cope effectively. Men are competitive. It's the way they were created. Their more aggressive nature may put you in situations where you have to choose whether to let it bother you or to roll with the punches.

Despite all the gallant efforts toward equality by corporate human resource officers, it's still up to women in the workforce to decide whether to be ultrasensitive and let their emotions hang out or simply relax and choose not to be easily offended. Thinking twice about the kind of relationship you want with your male colleagues will determine how you conduct yourself at work.

A Smart Girl knows how to take a joke and enjoy a joke. That doesn't mean she puts up with sexual innuendos or demeaning comments. It does mean that she can take a joke about herself, laughs freely with the men and women she works with, and generally maintains a good-natured perspective about office politics and the pecking order that exists in all work environments.

At the same time, you want to be wise about risking your heart and your reputation by becoming overly friendly with male coworkers. If there's a wolf on the prowl, the Smart Girl takes steps to evade him. If an occasion requires a meeting outside the office, she makes sure other women will be there. She avoids working late alone with any male coworker. Setting and following such guidelines may seem prudish, but it will protect you from more dangers than you may ever fully recognize.

Time spent in the workplace usually consumes a good chunk of your day, so finding a way to respectfully get along with the guys is a worthwhile priority. Of course, it can be just as challenging to get along with the girls, but we'll save that discussion for another time. Smart Girls who can get along respectfully with the men in the office usually can get along respectfully with the women. It's all about attitude.

Listen More Closely to His Actions than to His Words

Women are naturally more facile communicators than men. It's that brain thing again. Newborn baby girls show an awareness of the cries of other babies. They turn toward a face and focus sooner and for a much longer time than their baby boy counterparts.[3] Because of our own sensitivity to verbal communication, we women tend to take as fact the verbal cues we receive from men. But Smart Girls know that they protect themselves from painful situations when they evaluate a man by what he does, not by what he says.

Beware the Smooth Talker

One of the first men I dated seriously was blessed (or cursed) with the ability to speak with great fluency. He was an easy talker, full of fun, always ready to do meaningful things on the spur of the moment. One Sunday he came to my dorm to pick me up for church and said, "I have a surprise for you." Instead of going to the local church, we drove about fifty miles to a wonderfully quaint church tucked among huge pecan trees in a small southern town. The whole place was incredibly beautiful. The service was reverent, and the experience was memorable. My date gushed about this "shared experience." His words said, "I'm interested in the same things you are, and this gives us a special connection."

> A wise woman puts a grain of sugar into everything she says to a man, and takes a grain of salt with everything he says to her.[4]
>
> —HELEN ROWLAND

Soon after, I left town for a summer job with the full expectation that our relationship would continue. He had said, "We're in this together" and assured me that his love was true. A few weeks into our separation, however, I began to hear reports of his dating around. He made it convenient for himself and started dating a girl I had been rooming with. He could pick her up at the same address where he had collected me! The ironic thing was that his words never changed. Even after they were engaged, I continued to receive letters from him that made Lord Byron, the poet, sound tongue-tied. His words were tender and sweet, but they were not true. His behavior revealed who he was.

Because we realize that men's actions often reveal the truth more accurately than their words, Smart Girls know that the common practice of "trying out" marriage before exchanging vows is rank foolishness on the part of women. God created marriage to be the sole relationship involving sexual union, and the lure of sexual intimacy used to be one of the main motivations for getting married. These days, our culture has made sex such a casual interaction that marriage has been diminished to a "have to" instead of a "want to" for many men. How many women living with men are waiting for marriage proposals that never come? How many are raising children alone because sex came before the papers were signed?

The nature of the male (unless he is a changed man under God's power) is to avoid commitment. If a woman freely gives herself to a man, there's no reason he should marry. From the perspective of his male brain, he has nothing to gain and everything to lose. Marriage traps him financially and curbs his roaming. So if he can have sex with you without the vows, why wouldn't he?

Of course, worthy men know the value of marriage, home, and a long-term relationship. A good man will commit and stick to his word when he encounters a good woman he wants to spend his life with. A Smart Girl sees this and will value her relationship with such a man. She knows that God's plan for purity before marriage provides protection for the relationship and particularly for her. She knows that the woman sets the standard for the relationship, and she refuses to give away her bargaining power, preferring to take a chance on losing a man rather than give in to pressure for sex. She knows that if he won't commit to her without sex, she has little reason to trust him to remain faithful through years of marriage.

Don't Get Tangled Up with Fools

Women often learn, to their sorrow, that persuasive charmers are fools disguised in a pretty package. Of course, we all are capable of foolish behavior at times, but women need to be particularly careful around men whose behavior suggests a lifestyle of foolishness.

Such people will do whatever it takes to get what they want, and once they attain their objective, the trap slams shut.

I have worked with many women who have found themselves in the clutches of a male fool, whether a brother, father, husband, or tragically, even a son. Whatever the relationship, trying to relate to a fool is futile. Browse through the following verses from Proverbs and see if you can recognize any of these behaviors from one of the men in your life.

> A fool has no delight in understanding,
>> But in expressing his own heart. (18:2 NKJV)

> A fool's mouth is his destruction,
>> And his lips are the snare of his soul. (18:7 NKJV)

> It is honorable for a man to stop striving,
>> Since any fool can start a quarrel. (20:3 NKJV)

> There is desirable treasure,
>> And oil in the dwelling of the wise,
>> But a foolish man squanders it. (21:20 NKJV)

> Do not speak in the hearing of a fool,
>> For he will despise the wisdom of your words. (23:9 NKJV)

> Though you grind a fool in a mortar with a pestle along with crushed grain,
>> Yet his foolishness will not depart from him. (27:22 NKJV)

Fools of any stripe are extremely difficult to deal with, and it takes a lot of wisdom and grace to maintain your equilibrium in their presence. When it comes to relating to such people, all you can hope for is to find an arrangement that protects you from further harm. My suggested formula for dealing with a foolish man is to detach, feed him with a long-handled spoon, and pray! Simply explained: you need to protect yourself emotionally. Pull up the drawbridge as we discussed in chapter 6. Be kind but keep your distance. Don't allow yourself to be snared in his emotional trap. Pray and ask God for the guidance you need to be wise and innocent as you deal with the issues surrounding the behavior of a fool.

Look for Love in Action

As with bad behavior, a man's positive conduct speaks volumes and means just as much, if not more, to a Smart Girl than all the loving words he can string together. Since words are not generally a man's strongest way to communicate (again, there are exceptions), it pays to give attention to the consistent, kind, thoughtful things a guy does. Many women long for sweet words while they fail to notice and appreciate the kind actions of the men in their lives.

For example, the men in my family—my husband and three sons—are not what I would call sensitive communicators. They are men. They respect my position as wife and mother, but they have never been given to affectionate outbursts. My birthday and Mother's Day cards from them are funny, rarely sentimental. Our family times resemble locker room meetings, and sometimes I feel like the lone female reporter assigned to listen to their game-day victory chants. They freely kid among themselves and don't mind kidding me.

If I depended solely on their words to tell me that I am loved and appreciated, I could be starved for affection. Their actions, however, lavish me with love. They are attentive to any need I might have, are protective of our family and my position in it, and quickly arrive on the scene to take care of any crisis or project that needs tending. I have learned to observe their actions and not get hung up on their words.

Small examples of their care speak to me of love and honor. My husband knows I love Perrier, so he keeps the garage refriger-ator stocked for me. If my supply gets low, he makes it his business to haul in another crate and fill the fridge so those lovely green bottles will be cold. My son David cleans my two aquariums every week and instructs me on how to keep my fish healthy. My son Jon is always avail-able to care for our dog and cat when we go out of town. He's great about stopping by the house to let out our dog, Pearl, if we're delayed from getting home in the evening. My son Aaron keeps my com-puter working, and he built and updates my Web page. Mushy, they are not! Dependable and kind? Absolutely. They are honor-able men, and I love every one of them. It's all about what they do, not what they don't say.

> Women speak because they wish to speak, whereas a man speaks only when driven to speech by something outside himself—like, for instance, he can't find any clean socks.[5]
>
> —JEAN KERR

You may have men in your life who are verbally expressive and who behave in wonderfully demonstrative ways. Such relation-ships are great and can make it easier to connect emotionally with each other. If, however, you're feeling slighted because the family men around you are not great communicators, take heart and think twice. If their behavior is good, let it speak for them. Watch for the nonverbal ways they express their love, and let them know you appreciate their efforts. That's the sort of communication that makes life enjoyable.

Let Him Relax in His Own Way

The men in your life may be committed sports fanatics, or they may be into hunting, fishing, playing softball, running, computer games, or maybe even knitting. Whatever it is, they have their own way of relaxing—and it probably doesn't look anything like yours. It's easy to make a big deal out of the time a man spends on extra-curricular activities, but if he's found something he enjoys and it's not detrimental to your relationship or family, why not bless him when he does it?

Although our relational, communication-oriented, multitasking minds have trouble absorbing the fact that men actually do gain pleasure from certain activities, Smart Girls know that it's best to give guys space to do their thing, even if their chosen form of entertainment seems mindless and boring to us. I hasten to add that if an activity or hobby is consuming *all* his spare time, it would be helpful to talk things over. But if it's simply a pastime that helps him relax from the pressures of life, then it's best to just let him be, even if you don't understand the attraction. You'll receive more support for the pastimes you enjoy when you demonstrate a healthy tolerance level for the things he wants to do.

I remember with a combination of laughter and sadness the frustration that filled our house during so many Thanksgiving and New Year's Days of my childhood. Without fail, my mother would serve dinner in the middle of the biggest football game of the year. And every time my daddy, a dyed-in-the-wool football fan, responded by turning the big old console television at an angle where he could see the game from his seat at the dining-room table. Theirs was a silent war fueled by mutual exasperation. As a woman, she didn't appreciate his divided interest when it came to the big family meal she had prepared. Did he not understand all the work she'd put into preparing each dish and that we needed to eat while the food was hot? As a man, he resented her terrible timing in serving dinner in the middle of a game. Did she not understand that this game was a big deal to him and every other male guest who might be there? They each had their own perspective, and finding a compromise wasn't exactly their goal on those two days.

Now that I've discovered so much information about the brain, I can see that they processed the events in two different places in their brain structure. Had they known that, physiologically, they were viewing the situation through separate sets of lenses, maybe they would have been able to come to a mutual understanding. Then again, maybe not. But for me, understanding just a few facts about the male brain has allowed me to view those long ago holiday dramas—as well as my own husband's differing perspectives—in a softer light.

Self-Control Goes Both Ways

Another key area in which we need to understand the unique wiring of the male brain is that of beauty appreciation. It is a normal, natural thing for a man to enjoy looking at beautiful women. Smart Girls think twice about taking it personally because they know it's how men are designed, but they also know that an honorable man will curb his impulse to look as a matter of principle. Men will notice when an attractive woman walks by, but a man who respects you will not allow his gaze to linger.

I asked a young man who lives honorably with his wife what advice he would give to women on this topic. His almost immediate response was, "Men like to look at women, but it's like reading a menu with no intention to order. I would tell women not to overreact; it has nothing to do with you. But you also need to understand that a man who fails to consciously control his instinct to look at other women doesn't deserve your presence. And by the way, don't let him tell you he can't control the impulse. He can." I thought that pretty well summed up the issue.

A man's passing appreciation for a woman's beauty is not something to fight over. It's just something to be aware of. If you notice that a man you're dating tends to ogle every beautiful woman who comes by and keeps on ogling, you may want to move on to someone whose behavior is more respectful. If you're already married to a man who doesn't control his eyes, then a frying pan upside his head can redirect his gaze! Obviously I jest, but if you're feeling demeaned while your husband is feeling entitled, this is an issue that must be addressed. It does no good to fume quietly while your resentment builds. At the same time, the place to begin is not in ranting about his behavior but rather by exercising some self-control of your own and calmly telling your husband how you feel when he looks at other women longer than necessary. A quiet spirit will do more to win him than a raging confrontation. If the problem continues, talking with a third party whom you both trust could be helpful. If he refuses to go for counseling, then you can go to counseling on your own.

The Truth About Spiritual Influence

In thinking twice about how we relate to men, we do well to observe the biblical caution against developing too close an attachment with someone outside the faith: "Don't team up with those who are unbelievers. How can righteousness be a partner with wickedness? How can light live with darkness?" (2 Cor. 6:14). The answer to both questions, of course, is, "It can't." Ask anyone who has disregarded this warning, which is especially important for single women looking to marry one day.

For years, elders in the church have advised women, "Don't missionary date." Essentially, that's a warning against dating a guy in the hopes of influencing him spiritually. Some women naively believe that their virtuous example will lead an unbelieving man to desire a relationship with Christ. While I'm sure that some men have become Christians through the influence of a godly woman, many more have faked it to get the woman, creating a relationship based on deception.

Smart Girls know that feelings have a way of trumping good sense when it comes to falling in love, so they refuse to allow themselves to become emotionally involved with a man whose spiritual condition is questionable. Remember, the best way to really know what's in a man's heart is to watch his behavior. Words are cheap, and charm is deceitful. Only a man whose behavior is consistent and dependable deserves a second look.

Perhaps you're beyond the point of decision and already in a committed relationship with a man whose spiritual perspective doesn't match yours. Maybe you married believing he was a Christian, or maybe you found Jesus after you married, but he's not interested in joining you. Whatever the reason, if you are married to a man who is spiritually disengaged, whether or not he claims to be a Christian, the Bible's advice to you is pretty clear as well:

> In the same way, you wives should yield to your husbands. Then, if some husbands do not obey God's teaching, they will be persuaded to believe without anyone's saying a word to them. They will be persuaded by the way their wives live. Your husbands will see the pure lives you live with your respect for God. It is not fancy hair, gold jewelry, or fine clothes that should make you beautiful. No, your beauty should come from within you—the beauty of a gentle and quiet spirit that will never be destroyed and is very precious to God. In this same way the holy women who lived long ago and followed God made themselves beautiful, yielding to their own husbands. (1 Pet. 3:1–5 NCV)

The urge to do a little preaching and to drop hints about what you believe your husband should do can be nearly irresistible. Such methods might work for a man who wanted to attract his wife to the faith because women with a strong desire to please may respond to that kind of encouragement. But a man is a different animal, remember?

Tempting though it may be to believe that you can convince your husband of his need for a deeper spiritual life, your efforts are far more likely to prompt him to dig in his heels and refuse even to consider what God has to say. By demonstrating a quiet and sweet spirit as you treat your man with respect, you'll capture his attention more effectively than if you take it upon yourself to tell him what he needs to believe and how he needs to behave.

> A man would prefer to come home to an unmade bed and a happy woman than to a neatly made bed and an angry woman.[6]
> —MARLENE DIETRICH

Again, we have to remember that God created men quite different from us, so when He instructs us in Scripture to do something contrary to our nature—something as radical as keeping our mouths shut—it pays to listen. Following the admonition to nurture a gentle and quiet spirit requires a lot of trust. That's what being a believer is about: trusting God for the things that we can't see and can't figure out.

Whatever kind of men you're dealing with—whether relatives, acquaintances, or even your boss—remember that they are different. Their brains function differently, the way they process circumstances and events is different, but they are God's gift to us just as we are His gift to them.

Smart Girls know you gotta love 'em for who they are!

Chapter 8

All the Good You Can Do

Smart Girls Think Twice About Living Generously

People in my hometown still wear with pride their T-shirts proclaiming, "I Survived the Blizzard of '93." In Tennessee, snow in measurable amounts is a rarity, much less enough snow to qualify as a blizzard. But that time we were hit hard, and the area was practically paralyzed. Power lines were down all over the city. On our battery radio we heard the announcement, "If help hasn't come, it's not coming. Get all the quilts and blankets you can gather, go to a room in the middle of your house, and try to stay warm." People across the area were in great need. Since it was the week of spring break, the roads were packed with scantily clothed kids on their way to warm Florida beaches. Now the travelers were stranded on closed interstates.

But storms and other natural disasters have a way of sparking generosity, prompting us to take our eyes off our own problems and focus on meeting the needs of others. People living near major roads rescued hundreds with their all-terrain vehicles. Others delivered blankets and food to those who were trapped in their cars and unable to move. As in so many crisis situations, generosity was extended from stranger to stranger, and neighbors who barely knew each other became fast friends.

Heartwarming though such scenarios are, Smart Girls know that generosity and kindness aren't meant to be held in reserve for big storms or hard times. Generous living is an art to be practiced, a lifestyle that springs naturally from understanding that God really owns everything and we are merely conduits through whom He delivers His blessings. Once you grasp the concept that acts of generosity enrich you as much as they bless those on the receiving end, it's easy to hold loosely to what God gives you and joyfully pass it on to others. Generous living becomes a way of life.

Generous Living Is an Acquired Mind-Set

If we're paying attention, we'll notice examples of generosity and opportunities to express it—all around us.

My first lessons in generosity came through my daddy. We attended a church in downtown Washington DC where my dad kept some of the church records and usually could be found in the church office on Sunday mornings. I often stopped there to check in with him before the church service, and on more than one occasion, I found a shabbily dressed man sitting in the corner chair eating a sandwich. I don't know where my dad got the sandwiches and I was too young to understand all the circumstances, but it registered with me that when someone's hungry, the right thing to do is feed him.

Smart Girls have figured out that one of the reasons they were put on this earth is to be givers of God's goodness to other people.

139

Generosity isn't limited to money. A short note of encouragement, a basket of muffins, a flower left on someone's desk or doorstep, a surprise phone call, or a kind word in passing are all small generosities anyone can give. You don't have to have a lot, just the desire to share your time or skills or whatever God has blessed you with. Sometimes we forget all the tangible ways we can express God's love unless we've been in similar need ourselves. Providing a meal for a family whose mother is sick, volunteering to care for a friend's children while she goes to the grocery store, visiting someone who is confined in assisted living, offering a ride to someone who can't drive—all of these are physical offerings that require only your time, energy, and the willingness to be involved in someone else's life.

One of the most famous women in biblical history didn't have a lot, but she gave anyway and her generosity was noted for all time and eternity.

And [Jesus] looked up and saw the rich putting their gifts into the treasury, and He saw also a certain poor widow putting in two mites. So He said, "Truly I say to you that this poor widow has put in more than all; for all these out of their abundance have put in offerings for God, but she out of her poverty put in all the livelihood that she had." (Luke 21:1–4 NKJV)

This woman gave with total abandon. We don't know why she was such an ardent giver, but obviously her sacrificial gift was worthy of Jesus' attention. Although she had no money left, the widow didn't leave the temple that day expecting to die. She left ready to live in the confidence that God was her Provider.

Not long after this scene, Jesus challenged a crowd of people with some concepts that were way outside the box of their understanding. Remember, their culture held tightly to the old "eye for an eye and tooth for a tooth" philosophy. The idea of giving generously was a radical departure from what they had known. When it came time for tithing, their religious leaders meticulously measured out the spices to be sure they gave precisely one-tenth and not a pinch more. Jesus had strong words for these tightfisted givers: "How terrible for you, teachers of the law and Pharisees! You are hypocrites! You give to God one-tenth of everything you earn—even your mint, dill, and cumin. But you don't obey the really important teachings of the law—justice, mercy, and being loyal. These are the things you should do, as well as those other things" (Matt. 23:23 NCV).

> You will find as you look back upon your life that the moments that stand out, the moments when you have really lived, are the moments when you have done things in a spirit of love.[1]
>
> —HENRY DRUMMOND

So when Jesus challenged His followers to a new perspective on giving, the people listened with amazement to words like the following:

Give to everyone who asks you, and when someone takes something that is yours, don't ask for it back. Do to others what you would want them to do to you. If you love only the people who love you, what praise should you get? Even sinners love the people who love them. If you do good only to those who do good to you, what praise should you get? Even sinners do that! If you lend things to people, always hoping to get something back, what praise should you get? Even sinners lend to other sinners so that they can get back the same amount! But love your enemies, do good to them, and lend to them without hoping to get anything back. Then you will have a great reward, and you will be children of the Most High God, because he is kind even to people who are ungrateful and full of sin. Show mercy, just as your Father shows mercy.

Don't judge others, and you will not be judged. Don't accuse others of being guilty, and you will not be accused of being guilty. Forgive, and you will be forgiven. Give, and you will receive. You will be given much. Pressed down, shaken together, and running over, it will spill into your lap. The way you give to others is the way God will give to you. (Luke 6:30–38 NCV)

Did you notice that this whole discourse centers on the issue of heart attitude? Jesus didn't just toss out some rules for giving and leave it at that. The people already had rules and found them to be a burden. So Jesus spoke to them about love, mercy, and forgiveness. It's impossible not to give when our hearts and lives have been touched by God's love. Because we've acquired God's mind-set on generosity, we give as He calls us to give and expect nothing in return.

Where and How Is God Calling You to Give?

I truly believe that God tugs at our hearts to meet the needs He has prepared for us to meet. On occasion I've heard a request or observed a difficult situation but felt absolutely no compulsion to respond. Others may be passionate about giving to those people and places, but I just don't feel the call. At other times, a mere glimpse prompts me to make a U-turn. I feel compelled to go back and investigate. In such situations I always go with the intent to do whatever I can to meet the need God reveals because I know, for that moment in time, generosity is my assignment.

Two years ago I was driving down one of our winding Tennessee back roads on a sunny but biting cold December day. As I rounded a curve, I noticed a woman pushing a toddler in an umbrella stroller on the precariously narrow shoulder of the road. Ten or so feet behind her trudged a young man wearing a medium-weight jacket, his bare head bent into the wind.

Although I was headed the opposite direction and had plans for the morning, I knew without a doubt that I just couldn't keep going. I quickly found a driveway and turned around. I drove by the woman and pulled across the road from her. "Can I give you a ride?"

She looked both ways, then pushed the stroller in my direction. Her baby boy clearly was well nourished and absolutely beautiful, but his jacket was very thin and his little hands were red with cold. He had no hat, and there was no blanket across his chubby little legs. He had the typical runny nose of a toddler—and a killer smile.

> It is in giving that we receive.
>
> —ST. FRANCIS OF ASSISI

The woman told me where they were going, then her husband sprinted up and introduced himself as John. While his wife and baby settled into the back seat, John jumped into the front passenger seat and we began to get acquainted. I soon learned that the baby's name was Sebastian, and the family were refugees from Hurricane Katrina. They were staying at a hotel about four miles down the road while they tried to settle into our community. On this day they were headed to a house where John was being paid to cut down a tree. By the time I learned all this, we were almost to their destination. Convinced this meeting wasn't just about a half-mile ride in my car, I quickly began to gather facts. I asked what room they were staying in at the hotel, if they needed a ride back there later, if that was the only jacket the baby had, and did they need coats for themselves? "We're in room 146. That's Sebastian's only coat. No ma'am, we don't need coats for ourselves. We don't need another ride. We'll be fine." They scrambled out of the car after a round of thanks, and we parted.

Late that afternoon, I called the motel and asked for room 146. When the young woman answered, I asked if they had any urgent needs.

"Well, the baby could use some clothes, but John and I are fine."

I mentioned that Christmas was just around the corner. "Do you have any toys for Sebastian?"

"Yes ma'am, we bought him a toy. We're fine, really."

I hung up and immediately called Charlie. I quickly explained the situation and, gracious man that he is, my husband agreed to stop on his way home from work and pick up some size 2 baby boy clothes. Later that day he came in the door with several outfits and two jackets for Sebastian—one for very cold weather and one for not-so-cold weather. He also had bought a big yellow truck.

That evening I delivered the clothes and truck to the motel room. The young couple and their toddler came out to my car in their flannel jammies with white socks on their feet. The door to their room was cracked, so I could see a tiny—I mean *tiny*—lighted Christmas tree on the bedside table. As they thanked me profusely, husband and wife were smiling from ear to ear. They said FEMA had found them an apartment, and they would be moving in the next day or two. They hoped to get jobs near the apartment since they didn't have a car.

Although I tried to check in with them later, I never saw that dear family again—but I believe they were my assignment for that cold December day. I was a conduit of God's love to them for that time and that place.

I have come to recognize that my assignments often involve giving whatever I can to people in tight spots and lowly situations. I usually keep extra cash on hand for whatever comes up, and when I see such a person, I know that what I have is meant to go to them. I don't always know what happens after I give, but I don't have a choice. When God throws a need in front of me, I'm compelled to do whatever is called for in response to that assignment.

Some people are horrified at that style of random giving. Several years ago, as I rode with a ministry associate to an office where we had some business to conduct, I felt the unmistakable conviction that I was to give what I had to a man standing nearby. As soon as we pulled into our parking space, I jumped out of the car and gave the man some money wrapped in a little tract that explained how to have peace with God through Jesus Christ.

As my colleague and I entered the building, I noticed she was very quiet. I asked if there was a problem. She said, "I just can't believe you give money away like that." She found it troubling that I hadn't given it more forethought and perhaps done some investigating, yet I know her to be a very generous giver. I believe that neither of us was wrong; we simply have different approaches to giving.

When a need calls my name, I want to do what I can as soon as I can. Others are long-term planners who see that their money can be planted like seeds and yield a harvest down the road. It takes both kinds of generosity to get God's jobs done, and I do believe He is the one that puts it in our hearts to give. Knowing which style of giving fits your assignments requires knowing yourself and how you are wired to give.

Actively Seek Opportunities to Be Generous

Jesus instructed His followers, "Do to others as you would have them do to you" (Luke 6:31 NIV). This statement, known as the Golden Rule, is active, positive, and infused with a spirit of generosity. Similar guidelines in other religions are phrased in the negative: don't do to someone else anything you wouldn't want to have done to yourself. The focus is on what you refrain from doing rather than on what you actively choose to do.

The simple avoidance of causing harm to others can be summed up in the "live and let live" philosophy that is so much a part of our culture. But to actively seek opportunities to be generous and to give to people we don't know, or might not even care to know, is another story.

One Smart Girl I've known and admired for years is Anne Carter, a registered nurse who accompanies her surgeon husband, Lewis, to remote mission hospitals all over the world. Anne could have a quiet suburban existence with all the amenities. She could be at home, going to lunch with friends and enjoying her grandchildren, but she finds delight and joy in meeting the needs of others through her work in an African bush hospital.

> The very essence of Christian conduct is that it does not consist in not doing bad things, but in actively doing good things.[2]
>
> —WILLIAM BARCLAY

Many months out of the year, Anne and Lewis travel to remote places, offering people access to surgical procedures that otherwise would not be available to them. Lewis uses his skills to help burn victims and to repair cleft palates in little babies. Anne sacrificially works from early morning to late at night, using her ingenuity to deal with obstacles that would never come up in an American surgical suite. The work is grueling, but Anne delights in bringing improbable solutions to seemingly impossible situations. One year she learned they were scheduled to work in a remote hospital with no anesthesiologist. Though she usually serves as Lewis's scrub nurse, Anne threw her energies into learning how to anesthetize before she left the States. She trained intensively with two doctors for two months, and then she took more training to learn how to work with the antiquated machines she would encounter at their destination.

Anne has determined, with God as her source of strength, to cope with whatever situation comes her way so that she can extend hope to the hopeless. And the best thing is that she and Lewis get to tell those they treat about a relationship with Christ. Their generosity of spirit and great love for people allow them a listening audience. She comes home full of stories and bubbling with pleasure over the physical and spiritual needs they've been able to meet. Anne is a generous Smart Girl who wouldn't trade her life for any other.

Asking God to open your eyes to how you can live generously will send you on a journey you never will forget. In fact, the simple prayer "Show me what you want me to give today" may take you places and give you insights you would never discover on your own. Or God may use you close to home, prompting you to give in ways that never before occurred to you.

Irby, a good friend of our family, has struggled with acute kidney disease for many years. Early this year he found himself in need of something he couldn't buy, even if he'd had all the money in the world. He needed a new kidney. Several years ago, his cousin had given him a kidney, but it was now failing. Without a new kidney, he would have to go on dialysis several days a week. Lois, a dear woman in our church family, volunteered to give him one of her kidneys. She's strong and healthy and had been planning to give Irby her kidney if he ever needed another transplant. She didn't mention it to him, but as soon as word got out that he was looking for a donor, she contacted his doctor to see what the procedure would be. She was tested to see if her kidney would be a suitable match. Not surprisingly, it was exactly what Irby needed. Now our two friends from different families share in common the gracious giving and receiving of a kidney. Irby and Lois are a walking picture of the effects of generous living.

Great kindness pours forth out of a heart that has learned "it is more blessed to give than to receive" (Acts 20:35). Giving is a glorious adventure, and I encourage you not to be sidetracked on dreary byways by failing to catch a glimpse of what it's all about. In fact, you can make the journey even more enjoyable by inviting others along.

One Smart Girl I know saw the opportunity to help a bright young woman get through college. She couldn't handle the expense by herself, so she contacted some of her friends and told them about the need. Together they paid this young woman's way and saw her graduate. The benefactor didn't have to take on that project. It was just something that she wanted to do, and she joined her limited resources with those of others to make it happen.

Many people find great pleasure in sponsoring children through World Vision and other organizations that provide support for children in need. A great way to involve your family is to look through the files of such an organization and sign up to sponsor a child who shares your child or grandchild's birthday. Together you can embrace the joy of giving as you watch your sponsored child grow. I recently became the sponsor of a sweet little girl born in 2000, the same year as two of my grandchildren. I recently gave the picture of little Pili as a birthday gift to one of the children. I want my grandchildren to know that some children such as Pili, who have no parents, need generous people to help them survive. I pray that getting to know this precious child in Africa will help them understand the delights of being generous.

Let Wisdom Guide Your Generosity

Smart Girls don't give foolishly or without a sense of purpose. They want to be good stewards of God's blessings, so they think twice about scenarios in which they don't have much information about to whom they're giving. When you have a heart of mercy and a desire to help others, you want to be alert to situations that call for caution. If you're approached about a need that seems questionable, you may want to consult someone at your local church. Many congregations have a benevolence committee that provides a screening process for people who request assistance.

Working through a church or established organization also can protect you from awkward situations in which you feel pressured by the person in need or become uncomfortable about how your gifts are being used. Sometimes you need the fresh perspective of a trustworthy advisor to distinguish between genuine needs that arise from a temporary situation and those that signal a lifestyle of unhealthy dependence on others.

Harriett is a sharp woman, but her tender heart has led her into situations in which others take advantage of her. She recently learned a difficult lesson about wisdom in generosity after befriending a young married couple who said they wanted to be missionaries. She invited them to live with her while they raised support, and she encouraged her friends to offer financial assistance as well. In the meantime, the couple didn't bother to look for even temporary work. They just seemed to piddle away their days working on the computer, sleeping, and enjoying Harriett's hospitality. As the money began to accumulate, so did their excuses as to why they weren't ready to leave for the mission field. Finally, several of her friends began to question when the young couple was going to leave, and it dawned on Harriett that she wasn't doing them any favors. Her generosity had become a burden to their character and spiritual development. So she mustered the courage to set a deadline for their leaving her home and gently encouraged them on their way. After several false starts they eventually left, only to move in with another couple who was supporting them.

These people are takers, able-bodied individuals who could do something for themselves but choose not to—and they don't really have to because the givers in their lives just keep giving. Takers will milk another person's generosity for all they can get. Whether it's a family member, a friend, or a complete stranger you've hoped to help, giving becomes a burden when the taker won't do her part to break the cycle of need. To continue to give in such situations just keeps the merry-go-round twirling. This can be true in any situation where you're asked to give, whether you're donating time or money or supplies.

It is not always easy to answer objectively the ethical question of whether you are doing more harm than good by continuing to give. This is where you have to ask God about it. Talk to Him about what you see, how you're feeling about the situation, and what He wants you to do. If He leads you to see that your giving is not good for the taker, if your generosity has created a lifestyle of dependence rather than extending a temporary lifeline, it's time for your giving to cease.

The parable of the Good Samaritan points to the essential characteristics of wise giving. Jesus told the story in response to a man who was having trouble wrapping his mind around what it meant to love his neighbor as himself. Read it through and watch for the wisdom this good man showed at every step of his interaction with the man in need.

Then Jesus answered and said: "A certain man went down from Jerusalem to Jericho, and fell among thieves, who stripped him of his clothing, wounded him, and departed, leaving him half dead. Now by chance a certain priest came down that road. And when he saw him, he passed by on the other side. Likewise a Levite, when he arrived at the place, came and looked, and passed by on the other side. But a certain Samaritan, as he journeyed, came where he was. And when he saw him, he had compassion. So he went to him and bandaged his wounds, pouring on oil and wine; and he set him on his own animal, brought him to an inn, and took care of him. On the next day, when he departed, he took out two denarii, gave them to the innkeeper, and said to him, 'Take care of him; and whatever more you spend, when I come again, I will repay you.' So which of these three do you think was neighbor to him who fell among the thieves?"

And he said, "He who showed mercy on him."

Then Jesus said to him, "Go and do likewise." (Luke 10:30–37 NKJV)

We can gain several insights from this story of the wise and generous Samaritan.

First, the need was real. The man wasn't begging by the side of the road. He hadn't developed a lifestyle of being needy. This was a man genuinely injured in a surprise attack from thieves.

Second, the Samaritan was willing to divert his plans to help a stranger. He didn't ignore the man's plight because he was on a journey or because he didn't know the person bleeding there on the roadside.

Third, he got personally involved. The Samaritan didn't simply throw money at the problem, leaving a few coins with the injured man so he could pay the next traveler who came along to help him. He met the man's immediate needs by binding up his wounds, and then he took him to an inn and got him settled. Then the Samaritan gave sacrificially to cover the man's expenses and promised to pay whatever remained on the bill, if anything, on his return trip.

Fourth, after doing what he could, the good and wise giver went on his way. He didn't give up his trip to become overly occupied with the man's life. And he didn't become obsessed by the situation, worrying that he was the only one who could take proper care of the injured man.

Finally, the giver helped because he could, not because it would make him look good. To our knowledge, the Samaritan didn't announce to everyone how much help he had given to this man, nor did he condemn those who had ignored the man's suffering.

The Samaritan touched a stranger in need with the mercy of kindness, took him to a place of safety, and promised to check in on his way back through town. He gave what he could, when he could, and then he resumed his journey. That's healthy generosity.

Like the Samaritan, a Smart Girl gives generously but wisely. She doesn't give because it makes her feel good, although it is exhilarating to be of help. She doesn't give to be noticed or to ensure the strength of a relationship. She gives because she sees a need she knows she can meet. She gives because God, the great Giver Himself, has put it in her mind and on her heart to do so.

> The true services of life are inestimable in money, and are never paid. Kind words and caresses, high and wise thoughts, humane designs, tender behaviour to the weak and suffering, and all the charities of man's existence, are neither bought nor sold.
>
> —FROM *LAY MORALS* BY ROBERT LOUIS STEVENSON

Like the people who braved a blizzard and trudged through snow to take hot coffee, food, and blankets to a bunch of snowbound kids, we will sometimes encounter obvious opportunities to give generously. Other times the need may be more subtle. Either way, the question is whether we will be ready to recognize needs and respond or close up our hearts and keep what we have for ourselves.

The following quote from John Wesley deserves to be posted in a prominent place in the home of every Smart Girl committed to generous living. In fact, I would challenge you to put this on a three-by-five-inch index card and place where you'll see and read it daily: "Do all the good you can, by all the means you can, in all the ways you can, in all the places you can, at all the times you can, to all the people you can, as long as ever you can."

Chapter 9

Give Yourself a Break

Smart Girls Think Twice About Rest

W hen our boys were little, I occasionally would give them some Cheerios to eat, then settle them in front of the television while I collapsed on the sofa and tried to make up for what seemed like an insurmountable deficit of rest. Other days I would send the boys to their rooms and declare a period of "quiet time." In case you're of a spiritual mind-set, I should clarify that this was not a time for them to get in touch with God but simply an attempt to confine them long enough for their mother to get a much-needed break. If they didn't settle down immediately, I would plaintively call from the couch where I lay stretched out, "I am *trying* to rest." In reality, I probably expended more energy in *trying* to get some rest than I regained by these efforts. If you have children, you know the scenario.

"I am *trying* to rest." What an oxymoron! *Trying* and *resting* seem to be at cross-purposes. Yet isn't that exactly the problem many of us face? We really have to work hard at finding rest. It seems that the more responsibility we have, the more consciously we think about finding ways to *not* think about it. And the more we need rest, the harder we have to work at getting it.

Can you relate? Maybe you are trying to rest right now and wishing you could just drift off to sleep, but your body or your mind or your life just won't cooperate. I understand.

During certain seasons in our lives, it seems as if we will never again feel truly rested. In the early years of mothering, the constant demands of little ones make it hard to find a few minutes for yourself. Later, attending to the needs of aging parents or other older family members creates another sort of exhaustion. And sometimes we're dealing with it all at the same time: caring for babies and for grannies, working, driving the carpool, tracking teenagers, trying to keep a marriage healthy. There's always one more thing to do or one more person who needs our attention.

All of that leaves precious little time for us to kick back and relax. Yet rest is something Smart Girls actively pursue because we know that it deeply affects our quality of life.

Sleepy, Dopey, and Grumpy

Has sleep deprivation ever left you feeling groggy, foggy, and indifferent? Lack of rest not only affects us but those we love as well. A tired, worn-out demeanor can suck the luster right out of anyone in our vicinity, and our sleepiness can make us dopey and grumpy as we navigate life. When I was a teenager, I could sleep anywhere, anytime, for any length of time, yet the idea of sleep as a necessity of life never entered my mind. It wasn't until I became a mother and couldn't sleep whenever I wanted to that I realized how much rest matters—and how often life has a way of interfering. When things are rocking along on a day-to-day basis, we often find ourselves tempted to skimp on sleep. But in doing so we cheat ourselves and marginalize our physical, mental, and spiritual health.

In chapter 7, I mentioned how scientific studies are revealing more and more of what's going on inside our brains. Daniel Amen, MD, is one of the leading researchers looking into how we can make the most of our mental performance. Wonder of wonders, he and other researchers have determined that sleep is vital to a healthy brain. In fact, word is we need seven hours of sleep—count them, *seven* hours—per night to live optimally. Falling short of that will leave us with that dopey, grumpy feeling that we—and those around us—hate.[2]

> Sleep is a reconciling,
> A rest that peace begets.[1]
> —UNKNOWN

In addition Dr. Amen agrees with other researchers who say that the less we sleep, the more we weigh. Oh, gag. Now Dr. Amen has gone to meddling! "Sleep more, weigh less" would make a great bumper sticker, and you could add another that says, "Sleepy, Dopey, and Grumpy should have slept seven hours." The truth is, sleep is important. There's no virtue in forcing yourself to stay awake beyond the point where sleep deprivation begins to affect your brain function, which it will do![3]

Edna St. Vincent Millay was one of my favorite poets in high school. I always liked this little quatrain—probably because I could remember it!

> My candle burns at both ends
> It will not last the night;
> But ah, my foes, and oh, my friends—
> It gives a lovely light.[4]

Metaphorically, she paints a beautiful picture, but in reality pulling all-nighters is a delusional game we play with ourselves. The little work we're able to accomplish when we are tired takes longer than if we were rested, and it doesn't reflect our best thinking.

I was super tired a few nights ago. Although I should have turned in several hours earlier, I was determined to write just a little bit more. As I grew sleepier, the letters became blurrier. But I didn't spell-check, I just wrote. Finally I gave up, shut down the computer, and went to bed. The next morning, when I looked over my work, I thought, *Who on earth wrote this stuff?* It looked as if some deranged fairy had visited my computer during the night. Alas, it was only me burning my candle with a blowtorch!

Maybe you, too, have tried to squeeze just a bit more from a day than you should. But here's the truth: a life without rest means a brain under stress. A Smart Girl takes stress seriously and will be proactive about dealing with it by making sure her body gets plenty of rest. She views sleep as a priority, not something that waits until after she's checked everything else off her to-do list. Each day holds only twenty-four hours, and at least seven of those hours should be spent in sleep.

Because we as women are nurturing multitaskers, often we rationalize pushing the envelope when it comes to sleep. Somehow we talk ourselves into believing that if we can just get a project finished while everyone else in the house sleeps, then the time gained was worth the sleep lost. Occasionally that is true, but if we play that kind of game with our sleep on a regular basis, we damage our bodies. If you find yourself dragging, snapping, and wishing everyone would leave you alone, you might want to review your sleep schedule for the past few days and make some adjustments.

Smart Girls discover that unrealistic goals are, well, unrealistic and therefore need to be revisited. If you are trying to do more in a day than is humanly possible, could it be that some of those things don't have to be done? It really is okay to let yourself off the hook or to at least allow yourself a little more time to finish your project. No heavenly crowns are reserved for earthly superwomen. The myth that "you can do it all" is just that, a myth. You were not designed to do it all. You were created with a need for replenishment even in the midst of heavy assignments.

I have found that I cannot write a book and keep my little garden plot weeded. I look at the weeds, I look at my deadline, and I think, "Well, you little weeds just got a reprieve. Go ahead and grow, but when I've finished the book, look out. I'm coming to get you." I wish I had the Amazonian strength to do it all, including cooking those gourmet meals I see on the Food Network every night, but that isn't reality. There is a limit to what we can reasonably cram into one day, and Smart Girls honor it.

By the way, remember those sweet men we talked about in chapter 7? If you have one of those around the house, feel free to ask him to help out when you're in a bind. Remember, his brain doesn't work like yours, so on his own he probably won't see what needs doing. But if you ask him to help you out and maybe give him the specifics of what you need, you might be surprised at what he is willing to do. And kids can pitch in too. It's good for them to contribute to the household, and it's good for you to let go.

Often help is at hand but we fail to ask for it because of our own stuff. We talk ourselves into plugging along on our own with thoughts like *He won't do it right and I'll have to just go behind him,* or *I don't want to bother my kids with this; they have homework to do,* or *I don't want to ask a friend for a favor because the last thing I want to be is a moocher.* The problem is, our hesitancy to humble ourselves and ask for help, along with our obsessive need to do more than one human was ever intended to do, can take such a toll that we end up with deficient immune systems and many times just plain depressed. Smart Girls know that nothing is worth that, so they Stop, Look, Listen, and Look Again to see where they can lighten their daily load.

> Man is ill because he
> is never still.
>
> —PARACELSUS

Of course, there are times we're called on for hospital duty for a loved one or to help a friend through a crisis; such periods demand extraordinary grace and endurance. God rallies to our aid when we need Him, but He is not obligated to undergird us when we are just plain foolish about getting rest.

Putting Your Mind at Ease

Of course, setting aside time to sleep is just the initial step into the total rest of body, mind and spirit. Physical rest, mental rest, and spiritual rest are inextricably linked. Each flows from and into the others. For example, even when we set aside time for sleep, it can be difficult to get our brains and bodies settled in for a night's rest. Do you sometimes have trouble flipping the off switch of your mind?

Every Smart Girl knows herself and what helps prepare her mentally for sleep. I personally do not find praying to be a helpful sleep aid because my mind hops from one issue to another, and I just keep on talking to the Lord instead of going to sleep. For me praying is an important conversation with God, and I don't want to enter into it while planning to lull off to sleep in the middle. So I've learned that what works for me is to watch something mindless on TV. The sound of the TV and the nonintellectual stimulation distract me from thoughts that otherwise could keep me awake.

My friend Carolyn travels with me to many of my speaking engagements, and we usually share a room. Because sleeping in a strange place can make it hard to fall asleep, we purposed to work out a sleep routine that helps us drift off and also assures a successful night's rest. We routinely bring sound machines along to help block out any noises that could disturb us, especially me. I fall asleep easily but I'm a light sleeper who is easily awakened by the slightest noise. Carolyn, by contrast, needs time to settle down for sleep, but once she's out I don't think an earthquake would awaken her. So when we're ready for bed, she reads to settle down while I look at the TV. Once I'm out, she turns off the TV and turns on the sound machines. By then, she's ready to sleep herself. We laugh about being two little old ladies who are set in our ways, but this routine works for us. When it comes to sleep, I believe Smart Girls say, "Whatever it takes!"

Each woman has her own favorite brain-soothing sleep solution. I know people who use all kinds of mental relaxation rituals, such as drinking warm milk, reading, listening to music, sitting in total silence, drinking chamomile tea, spraying lavender on the sheets, or hugging a favorite pillow. And many people use melatonin as a great natural way to help their brain find its sleep rhythm. Watching the craziness of the late-night news, drinking a caffeinated beverage late in the day, or even eating something that might upset your digestion are all behaviors a Smart Girl can avoid.

None of these little tricks gives us true mental rest, however. They just short-circuit our brains so we can get physical rest. Sleep makes it easier to find mental rest, and mental rest leads to better sleeping patterns.

Resisting the Urge to "Awfulize"

Because body, mind, and spirit are so interrelated, genuine rest can be particularly elusive when you're feeling stressed about projects lingering on your to-do list or circumstances that are troubling your soul. Your ability to get mental rest—to let go of stress, tension, and the daily concerns that tend to jitter around in your brain—is highly dependent on your personal self-talk. Do you speak restful messages to yourself, or do you stir up troubling thoughts?

Dr. Marie Chapian, the remarkable woman you met in chapter 4, introduced me to the term *awfulizing*, which describes the habit of viewing just about everything that comes our way as perfectly dreadful. A friend doesn't call; a child doesn't perform well in school; a husband forgets an anniversary; a boss is grumpy; a coworker is sloppy; a tire goes flat; a water heater springs a leak; a new dog wets the carpet; an old cat coughs up a fur ball in front of company—the list goes on and on. All of these events are annoying, even disappointing, but they don't qualify as awful. Yet how easily our brains tend to run on an *awful* track that makes everything seem worse than it really is. If our personalities have any sort of negative bent, we can become habitual *awfulizers* whose thought patterns rob of us of our rest and peace. We all know that woman— maybe it's you!—who, when her husband is five minutes late getting home from work, can have him mentally dead and buried within three seconds flat and has formulated a plan for supporting herself as a widow before his tires hit the driveway. Some minds just naturally seem to go worst-case scenario and beyond without much effort.

Awfulizing keeps us keyed up with tension throughout the day, steals our peace in quiet moments, and prevents us from being able to truly rest—to cease from any mental or physical activity that requires energy. Certainly each of us will face some disappointing, difficult, tragic—perhaps truly awful—events in our lives, and our perspective in such circumstances will lead us either to peace-giving rest or to deeper distress.

Smart Girls know that rest comes only from realizing that what is already is, what's coming is in God's control, and thinking "how awful" won't change a thing.

When my mother began to fail rapidly and I couldn't get to her quickly because I was in a remote part of California, I was tempted to dwell on the awfulness of it all. My mind initially whirled with the thoughts that I should have been able to get there, it was awful that I couldn't, and any daughter who really loved her mother would have been able to find a way to make it happen. I could have allowed my thinking to continue down this long and winding trail, but when I learned that she had died while I was still a few hours away, I sought peace in trusting that God knew my heart and my effort. I'd done the best I could to get to her side, but I didn't make it. That was not awful. It was truth, but it wasn't awful truth. Disappointment over how it all happened still crops up in my mind occasionally, but I know that pursuing those thoughts will destroy my mental rest and I also know it would do absolutely no good to rehash all of that, so I have refused to go there.

Are you tormented by a situation that threatens your mental rest? Does it return to your mind on a regular basis and take away your peace? If so, I would encourage you to consider how you might be awfulizing the situation. Remember, viewing life through the darkened lens of dread will cause you to stumble off the pathway of peace.

Adjusting Your Perspective

Even those of us with a fairly positive outlook on life can find ourselves awfulizing when we compare ourselves and our lives today with what used to be. At forty, we may long for the seemingly carefree days of our twenties. At sixty, we gaze back at forty and realize how very young our bodies were and how little we appreciated them at the time. I can only imagine that the eighty-year-old looks at the sixty-year-old and thinks, *What a great age to be!*

> Regret for wasted time is more wasted time.[5]
> —MASON COOLEY

Since our view of life has a direct impact on our ability to rest, we'll find peace in remembering that every season of life brings both beauty and pain. To accept where you are at this moment and to fully embrace the joy of being alive today leads to a mental rest that nothing can disturb.

Taken together, the words of Psalm 1 and Psalm 92 present a composite portrait of the person who embraces her season. I encourage you to personalize these Scriptures and apply them to yourself, inserting your name and changing each pronoun to *she*, as I have done here. I think you'll be amazed at how the words nestle down into your heart and bring peace to your mind.

> But [your name]'s delight is in the law of the LORD,
>> And in His law she meditates day and night.
> She will be like a tree firmly planted by streams of water,
>> Which yields its fruit in its season
>> And its leaf does not wither;
>> And in whatever she does, she prospers. (Ps. 1:2–3 NASB)

> Righteous [your name] will flourish like the palm tree,
>> She will grow like a cedar in Lebanon.
> Planted in the house of the LORD,
>> She will flourish in the courts of our God.
> She will still yield fruit in old age;
>> She shall be full of sap and very green,
> To declare that the LORD is upright;
>> He is my rock, and there is no unrighteousness in Him.
>> (Ps. 92:12–15 NASB)

Just as meditating on truths like these in Scripture can adjust my outlook, I have learned that another way to proactively pursue mental rest is to put into practice the principle of "change one thing." When I'm feeling stuck in some distasteful circumstance, I find that changing just one thing can alter my view of the whole situation and, in time, may even alter my view of what's worth getting stressed about.

Most often the "one thing" I change is my view—literally. I take a minibreak and head outside to look around at what the birds are doing. Even in big cities there are busy little sparrows cheerfully chirping while they find their food. They have amazing radar for the crumbs people leave in parking lots. They love the bugs smashed into the grilles of cars that provide easy pickings. Big, messy pigeons blissfully survive by waddling around pecking at whatever is supplied to them on the ground. I've never seen a skinny pigeon!

Just looking at the birds settles my brain in a quieter place of rest, if only for a few minutes. I draw a deep breath, and somehow my stress is lessened and my mind can rest. Such scenes often bring to mind the words of Christ: "Look at the birds of the air, for they neither sow nor reap nor gather into barns; yet your heavenly Father feeds them. Are you not of more value than they?" (Matt. 6:26 NKJV).

Minibreaks like these are a great way to break into your routine and alter one thing, if even for a day. You can do what you like best. Make it pleasurable, make it relaxing, and make it your choice. One friend of mine occasionally takes a one-day "cruise" without leaving home. She pulls out the good chocolates, finds an engaging book, puts an atmospheric CD on the player, and disconnects the phones. She then takes the day to go for a mental cruise, taking a vacation from whatever distressing thoughts have been occupying her mind. She arrives at work the next day refreshed, rejuvenated, and ready to face the stuff of life from a new perspective.

There are other ways to change one thing. For example, I changed the way I read the Bible this year. My reading style had always been "here a book, there a book, everywhere a book, book," but this year I determined to change one thing by reading chronologically. It has opened up vistas of interest that I wasn't aware of before. I have seen God's workings with the sons of Israel in a whole new way, and that has opened my mind to new thoughts, new concepts, and new biblical tidbits that I had missed before.

Trust me, a little change opens doors to much bigger changes. Grabbing hold of what you can change, even if it's something minuscule, makes a difference in what happens in your brain. It proves that you aren't helpless. You may face limitations, but you can take charge of what you think and how you process your circumstances.

Trading Your Worries for God's Peace

We already have seen how fear and stress can destroy physical and mental rest. Since each aspect of our lives is interwoven, the haunting dread of fear and the palpitating tension of stress also will rob even the strongest Christian of her spiritual rest.

A Smart Girl knows that allowing fear and stress to consume her will only make a difficult situation worse. Emotional turmoil is absolutely natural in difficult situations, but when she can pull her thoughts together, she begins to rehearse the things for which she is thankful. That sounds like a strange antidote to the stress and fear that annihilate our rest and peace, but it's proven to be effective.

The new brain science has shown that an appreciative mind counteracts fear; in other words, gratitude and fear cannot be maintained in the same brain at the same time.[6] I have read, loved, and taught God's Word for years. I know that it is the guide for life, and its pages hold the secrets to living a vibrant life. I have known that God's ways work for His creatures; I just didn't know why. As I have read so many wonderful new studies on the brain, it has hit me as never before that God's Word has been telling us these truths for centuries. God, our Creator, mapped out the way to be at rest so long ago. He knew that to enjoy optimal living we would find it necessary to bring our minds under control and to proactively seek a remedy for fear and stress. For this reason God says through the apostle Paul in the book of Philippians, "Be anxious for nothing, but in everything by prayer and supplication, with thanksgiving, let your requests be made known to God; and the peace of God, which surpasses all understanding, will guard your hearts and minds through Christ Jesus" (4:6–7 NKJV).

Anxiety robs each moment of its richness and joy. As every moment moves on, why regret how you have handled it? Why live in the stress-producing shadow of would've, should've, could've? During moments when anxiety threatens to creep in, I grab hold of one of my favorite life mottoes. I already mentioned this in chapter 6, but I think it's worth repeating here: "What might have been does not exist. So don't even go there!" That is so, so significant. The land of What Might Have Been is a place of torment. You can't set foot on its soil without being anxious. I want never to go there—even by mistake.

Instead, I've learned to cling to one of God's most open secrets. Prayer and a grateful heart are the doorposts at the entrance to peace, and a relationship with Christ Jesus is the door. If you are in relationship with Jesus, then when stress of any kind threatens your rest, you can pray (talk to God about it) and give thanks and enter into the peace "so great we cannot understand it" (Phil. 4:7 NCV). What struck your heart with fear a moment before—or agitated your body with stress—will be under the feet of Christ's dominion when you give it to Him in prayer and thank Him for taking it. It's a miraculous exchange: His peace for your thankful heart. Your body benefits because your brain has been quieted. God is there.

When the Burden Seems Too Great
Sometimes the weight that pulls you down comes from more than a passing anxiety, fear, or stress. You are exhausted because of an ongoing trial or responsibility that you've carried on your shoulders,

not for days or months, but for years. Many women in the middle and senior years of life find themselves facing situations they never dreamed would be theirs.

I've watched a woman caring for a husband with a neurologically debilitating disease over the past several years. He can't do anything but sit in a wheelchair. He can't speak. He can't even smile. The disease has taken away any communication they might have had. She receives help from nurses, but the main responsibility of their situation is hers to bear. He was diagnosed twenty years ago. She promised him then, when they were in their early fifties, that she would care for him at home for as long as he lived. She has been true to her promise with a cheerful spirit, but you can only imagine how heavy her burden must be. Every day, he loses a little bit more of who he was. The man she loved has lost every way to tell her "thank you" or "I love you." He's still in there, but he can't reach out even to support her emotionally.

Christ addressed the needs of my friend and others in similarly exhausting situations when He said long ago, "Come to Me, all you who labor and are heavy laden, and I will give you rest. Take My yoke upon you and learn from Me, for I am gentle and lowly in heart, and you will find rest for your souls. For My yoke is easy and My burden is light" (Matt. 11:28–30 NKJV).

Maybe those words pour like cool water over your weary, parched soul. All of us will grow tired at times and need to be refreshed. In such circumstances Smart Girls know how to embrace the gift Jesus offers.

Let me slip on my teacher's hat for a moment. I love words, especially words with colorful, meaningful explanations. The New Testament is packed with such words because it was written in Koine Greek, an earthy, vibrant, descriptive language. By examining some of the words in this passage, we may uncover a blessing you didn't know was waiting, one of those secrets the Lord has planted in His Word for those willing to look a little closer at what may seem familiar.

The word used in Matthew 11:28 for *labor* describes extremely demanding labor, the kind that is both physically and mentally crushing. It requires your all. This isn't the sort of task that requires a little burst of energy and is soon over; it's true labor that goes on and on with no end in sight. Think of carrying a huge rock up a steep, arduous trail with unnumbered miles yet to go.

The word for *rest* comes from the Greek word *anapauō* and means "to pause, to cease, to desist." If you had to explain it in today's language, you might say it means to "get away, take a break, come up for air."

Jesus offers peace to the anxious and rest to the weary. But in the middle of each of those invitations is a caveat, an action you must take. When you are anxious, He says, "Pray and give thanks." When you are bone-tired weary, He says, "Come and take my yoke upon you."

He invites you to "yoke up" with Him. Can you visualize that? In this passage, as He so often did when making a vital point, Jesus was creating a mental picture for His listeners, but many of us aren't familiar with the imagery He used. "Take my yoke upon you" may not make much sense unless you've seen two farm horses hooked up to a plow.

I imagine that perhaps Jesus had in mind the oxen used as beasts of burden in Israel. For purposes of pulling a load, two such animals would be connected to each other by means of a single yoke, or wooden bar, that joined them at the head or neck. It was important that the yoke fit well so it wouldn't chafe or make it more difficult for them to pull their load. The yoke also kept the two animals going in the same direction. It hindered the wanderlust of self-willed oxen.

So with these words, Jesus was issuing an invitation to come to Him with your heavy load so that He can help you carry it. He has strength to share in your weakness. He has wisdom to share when you lack insight. When you find yourself crying out, "What do I do?" He says, "Yoke up with me. Let me pull alongside you, and you will find rest for your soul."

Smart Girls Don't Go It Alone

Plenty of people try to pull their own loads. They think it's a mark of valor to stoically handle by themselves whatever comes their way. They worry that sharing their burdens will require them to give up too much control, or they think that partnering with another just doesn't fit their style. Sadly, when they break down under the load, those who refuse to be "yoked" have nowhere to turn.

I have watched one particular woman resist Jesus' yoke for years. In her younger years she forged a path for herself through intelligence, skill, and manipulations. Now as an older woman she has the man, she has the money—and she thought she had it all. But several years ago she opened up to me about some difficult issues she was facing. I talked with her about yoking up with Jesus. After toying with the idea, she decided, "No, I don't think so. I can handle it." Then life handed her a burden that was way too heavy for her. She wanted to carry it alone but doubled over under the crushing force of its weight. She finally looked around for someone to help, but no human could offer her any assistance that would make a difference. She rejected Jesus' offer and was left broken and exhausted. She is sad and floundering even as I write this.

Independent-minded women may find it difficult to think of submitting to someone who is stronger and wiser and who may lead them down a different path than they would choose for themselves. But Smart Girls think twice about the consequences of self-reliance and recognize the payoff that comes with joining up with

Jesus. It's something they cannot buy or create or obtain from anyone except Him. That payoff is rest. The only requirements are to come to Him and submit to Him.

Jesus caps His invitation by saying, "For my yoke is easy and my burden is light." When we join with Him, He provides whatever is needed and the things He asks us to do are not hard. "Loving God means keeping his commandments, and his commandments are not burdensome" (1 John 5:3).

Is the payoff worth it for you to trust Christ enough to invite Him into your life? Can you allow Him to determine your path and to carry your burdens? That is a true yoking together that will change your life. That is the place you will find true rest.

> Like any other gift, the gift of grace can be yours only if you'll reach out and take it.[7]
>
> —FREDERICK BUECHNER

Maybe you already have asked Jesus to come into your life, but you're holding on to some person or some situation that keeps you bent down with anxious thoughts and stress. You can't fix the problem because if you could have, you would have. Or maybe your peace has shattered because you are pulling against Jesus, trying to go your own direction? If this is your situation, the Bible says, "Humble yourselves under the mighty hand of God, that He may exalt you in due time, casting all your care upon Him, for He cares for you" (1 Pet. 5:6–7 NKJV). *Casting* means "to hurl." You don't hurl something away that you intend to look for and reclaim. You hurl something far away expecting never to see it again. So it is with our cares. A Smart Girl knows that casting them all on Jesus is the most peaceful, stress-reducing, rest-enhancing step she can take. Only He has the power to transform our problems, cares, and issues into something that will work for good because we love Him.

By hanging on to whatever is disturbing our peace, we say to God, "I love you but . . ." What follows the *but* may be "I'm afraid to let go" or "I'm not sure I trust you" or "I think I have some pretty significant power on my own." It takes courage to humble ourselves enough to cast our burdens on Jesus and let Him direct our steps, but when we do, peace comes and God's pleasure will flow, in due time.

Chapter 10

Who Will You Trust with Your Life?

Smart Girls Think Twice About God

As a young wife and mother, I wrestled with a fierce fear of death. If I read a magazine article about the symptoms of a particular disease, I was convinced that I had it. Worse than that, if it happened to be an illness with any mortality rate at all, I just knew I was going to die. I was haunted by the fear that I would pass away before I could raise my sons. My deepest horror was that they might grow up as motherless children.

Now, I had been raised to know that there was a God and that Jesus was His only begotten Son, but beyond that I had never made the connection that God cared about me and that He was intimately involved in my life. I had no clue that everything in my life, good or bad, occurred under the direct, sovereign authority of the God I vaguely knew.

I had attended a good church that taught the Bible and encouraged its young people to have lives of service. Yet somehow, in spite of those advantages, I just didn't get it. I probably didn't feel a need to get it in those early years because life was rocking along pretty well.

Then my world began to take on new dimensions and dynamics. At age twenty-one I married Charlie, and at twenty-three I said good-bye to my young husband, who had become an officer in the army and was leaving to fly helicopters in the hot, dangerous jungles of Vietnam. We had a six-month-old baby, and I was fearful. The year that Charlie left, my life became more and more tremulous. We could communicate only through letters. No phone calls, no e-mail. My sole source of information about his situation was the nightly news, and it was never good.

Even as I worried over Charlie's chances of survival, I was on hyperalert about my own health. When I found a nodule in my thyroid gland for the second time in eighteen months and learned I needed surgery again, my head was dragging, and my heart was so depressed. My surgeon picked up on my self-pity and reminded me that this was not the end of the world. He wisely told me, "I operated on a young woman this morning whose husband is in Vietnam, and I don't believe she will live until he comes home. I really think you will be fine."

The nodule was benign, and Charlie and I both survived the year. When he finally came home, I thought everything would be good again. All I had wanted was for him to come back safely so we could take up where we'd left off, but it didn't happen that way. He was a changed man who had seen war up close and personal. I was a changed woman who wasn't sure what she wanted anymore. Within a few weeks of his return to the States, we had to leave for a new assignment. This meant we had to tear eighteen-month-old David away from my grieving parents, who by now had spent far more time with him than he'd spent with his daddy his whole life. I knew it was right to keep our little family together, but the pain of hurting my folks was very acute. Being older and wiser, they handled it better than I did. It nearly broke my heart.

We arrived at Fort Rucker, Alabama, to start a new life as two changed people. I was soon pregnant and very depressed, and my young husband was making the difficult transition from warrior to husband. After eight lonely, almost desperate months at Rucker, we moved to Chattanooga, where Charlie had a job waiting with the Tennessee Valley Authority. Two weeks after we moved, our second son, Jonathan, was born. We settled into doing life, but before long fear once again took over my life.

This was when my heart began to palpitate with panic that I would die and my little boys would be left motherless. I couldn't shake the sense of impending doom. What I couldn't see was that God was setting the stage for an encounter with Him. In my daily thoughts, I wanted to know there was a reason for our life circumstances. I wanted to know that there was a God who really cared. I could repeat the gospel, but I didn't understand its correlation to my life. With a weary, confused mind, I sought an answer to the fears that gripped me. I tried reincarnation, but that wasn't it. I tried Unitarian Universalism, but that wasn't it. I already knew that being a member of my home church wasn't the answer because that, too, had left me empty. Deep in the core of my being, I longed to discover the truth about God. I had to know just who He was and if He truly cared about me. Even more significantly, I had to know that I could trust my children's lives into His care.

> God alone is our true good.
>
> —BLAISE PASCAL

I wasn't a Smart Girl. I was a lonely, lost, clueless, young woman, overwhelmed by life's responsibilities. Then God stepped in. Though I'd been looking for Him, I didn't have much hope of finding Him. I didn't know that the Bible promised, "Ask, and God will give to you. Search, and you will find. Knock, and the door will open for you. Yes, everyone who asks will receive. Everyone who searches will find. And everyone who knocks will have the door opened. (Matt. 7:7–8 NCV).

God met me in a church service on a Sunday night in September. I was sitting in the balcony when I heard the words that changed me forever. A singer named Jo Ann Shelton was giving a concert. She stopped in the middle of it and told some of her story. She said, "All my life I played games with God, and then I had to get serious." Those words pierced my very being. I knew who God was, but I didn't know Him. I had been playing games, trying to find out who He was, and I hadn't even realized it. So that night I gave everything I knew of me to everything I knew of Him. Because of my church background, I probably knew more about Him than I knew about me. I was so confused about my marriage, about my life, and about the fears that haunted me.

That night in 1971 my life began to change in all kinds of small ways, but the most important change was that I began to know God. I took a second look at His character and heart as revealed in the Bible and recognized that I'd missed some things while I was playing at trying to find Him. In my struggle with the fears that consumed me, I'd completely missed the truth that God loves me, and He's the answer to every overwhelming emotion or situation we will ever have to face.

That's how my journey with God began. Do you remember when your journey started? Or are you still waiting to start the journey because you're unsure who or what you can trust? Oh my, do I understand. That's why I'd like to tell you about some of the things I've learned about God and why I've traded in my quivering fear for unshakeable trust.

God Is Sovereign

One of the best truths I have learned is that you and I can control nothing; God controls everything. That's the best news you will ever receive because when you get to know God, you'll discover that He is lovely, kind, wonderful, and trustworthy. He holds your life in the very palm of His hand. Absolutely nothing slips God's notice or His concern. He is the Creator of all that is, and He rules over all that He has made. That means you don't have to keep trying to hold everything together. In fact, you'll never be able to grasp what God has for you if you insist on holding on to the things you think you can control.

Throughout history He has worked through the children of Israel to prove to the world that He is God. He chose the nation of Israel to be His people, and He prepared a land for them—the Promised Land. When you read His dealings with them, you see His sovereignty and His might. Take a slow walk through the following words from Deuteronomy 4 and see what you learn about the rulership of our God.

> He showed you things so you would know that the LORD is God, and there is no other God besides him. He spoke to you from heaven to teach you. He showed you his great fire on earth, and you heard him speak from the fire. Because the LORD loved your ancestors, he chose you, their descendants, and he brought you out of Egypt himself by his great strength. He forced nations out of their land ahead of you, nations that were bigger and stronger than you were. The LORD did this so he could bring you into their land and give it to you as your own, and this land is yours today.
>
> Know and believe today that the LORD is God. He is God in heaven above and on the earth below. There is no other god! (vv. 35–39 NCV)

And in Daniel 4:35, we see the breadth of His power. There is no place that His sovereign rule does not reach.

> All the inhabitants of the earth are reputed as nothing;
>> He does according to His will in the army of heaven
>> And among the inhabitants of the earth.
> No one can restrain His hand
>> Or say to Him, "What have You done?" (NKJV)

The sovereign God described in these verses not only chose the children of Israel but He chose us as well. Let the wonder of these words from 1 Peter 2 flow down over you and refresh your being like cool water on a hot day.

> But you are a chosen people, royal priests, a holy nation, a people for God's own possession. You were chosen to tell about the wonderful acts of God, who called you out of darkness into his wonderful light. At one time you were not a people, but now you are God's people. In the past you had never received mercy, but now you have received God's mercy. (vv. 9–10 NCV)

I love those words. I can never get enough of reading that we are "a people of God's own possession." I have heard it explained like this: if you draw a large circle and put a dot in the middle of that circle, you have just demonstrated God's relationship to us. We are surrounded by a God who loves us supremely and encircles us with Himself. Nothing comes to us without passing through Him.

For me, with my fear of illness and death, the truth of God's sovereignty brought incredible relief. I could know that nothing would take Him by surprise, nor would anything get to me without His control. It also occurred to me that God's circle of possession was around my boys. I found daily comfort in the sweet words of Psalm 138:8: "The LORD will accomplish what concerns me; Your lovingkindness, O LORD, is everlasting; do not forsake the works of Your hands" (NASB). The word *accomplish* comes from the Greek word meaning "completion." So the wonderful news for my troubled soul was that not only was I right in the middle of the circle of God's possession, but He also promised to bring to completion all that concerned me. My boys, my marriage, my life, even my fears—all lay within His control, and He was in the business of finishing everything about me.

Wow. What great news for you and me. As we release ourselves into His hands, taking our eyes off our stuff so we can give Him the second look He deserves, we become the solid, strong, and secure Smart Girls we long to be—because of Him!

God Cares About His People

When God dealt with the children of Israel, He protected them like an eagle caring for His young. Because we also are "a people for God's own possession" (1 Pet. 2:9 NCV), part of His chosen because of our belief in Jesus (Eph. 2:11–16), He hovers over us with the same concern. Drink in this incredible picture from Deuteronomy 32:

> The LORD took his people as his share,
> the people of Jacob as his very own.
> He found them in a desert,
> a windy, empty land.
> He surrounded them and brought them up,
> guarding them as those he loved very much.
> He was like an eagle building its nest
> that flutters over its young.
> It spreads its wings to catch them
> and carries them on its feathers.

The LORD alone led them,
and there was no foreign god helping him. (vv. 9–12 NCV)

God, the mighty eagle, cares for His young with an intense interest. He watches and when they are big enough to leave the nest, He stirs it up, forcing them to get out and fly. But He is always ready to catch them on His strong feathers if their weak little wings should fail. That's how God cared for His people, Israel, whom He loved, and He will do the same for you and me, whom He loves just as much.

> God loves to show off his greatness by being an inexhaustible source of strength to build weak people up.[1]
>
> —JOHN PIPER

You may be saying, "Well, how can I know that He loves me? I don't always feel it." I understand, but when we recall what He has done for you and me, there is no rational explanation but love. And besides, He not only has said He loves us but He also has shown us. "God loved the world so much that he gave his one and only Son so that whoever believes in him may not be lost, but have eternal life. God did not send his Son into the world to judge the world guilty, but to save the world through him" (John 3:16–17 NCV).

God sent His Son, Jesus, to let us know that He loves us, just as He showed Israel in so many ways that they were loved and that He could be trusted. He never stops being the Supreme Ruler of the Universe, and He never gives up His role as the great Lover of our souls.

God Is the Highest Power—Not Just a Higher Power

Several years ago after one of my speaking events, I was confronted by a young woman who took exception to my statement that there is only one God and He is the God of the Bible, the God of Abraham,

Isaac, and Jacob. In a challenging tone she asked, "What difference does it make who my Higher Power is? If I want to worship a doorknob, what difference does it make?" The answer seemed obvious to me, but to someone who didn't want to be limited in her choice of "Higher Powers," her question made perfect sense. The idea of choosing your own Higher Power resonates with a person who doesn't know the God of the Bible. To know Him is to recognize that there is no other Higher Power and also that no lower power is able to meet the deep needs of your soul. That's a difficult concept for us—humanity in general—to grasp.

The attraction to gods of our own choosing is an ancient dilemma. The Old Testament offers detailed and compelling descriptions of God, often revealed through the prophets who spoke to His people about Him and for Him. The prophets tried to explain what was on God's heart and mind to a people who felt drawn to create their own gods. Their behavior is really no different from our own tendency to turn to gods we think we can control. Their idolatry just seems a little simpler and more blatant—although worshiping a doorknob is fairly simple and blatant, come to think of it.

The prophet Isaiah wrote these words to the children of Israel, the people of God's own possession in whom we can see ourselves.

> Can you compare God to anything?
>> Can you compare him to an image of anything?
> An idol is formed by a craftsman,
>> and a goldsmith covers it with gold
>> and makes silver chains for it.
> A poor person cannot buy those expensive statues,
>> so he finds a tree that will not rot.
> Then he finds a skilled craftsman
>> to make it into an idol that will not fall over.
>> (Isaiah 40:18–20 NCV)

Then Isaiah added this:

> God, the Holy One, says, "Can you compare me to anyone?
>> Is anyone equal to me?"
> Look up to the skies.
>> Who created all these stars?
> He leads out the army of heaven one by one
>> and calls all the stars by name.
> Because he is strong and powerful,
>> not one of them is missing. (40:25–26 NCV)

I have heard dear, dear people say "Oh, I believe in a Higher Power." I want to say, "Oh, I know you think you do, but if you really know the God who created the Universe, He will be more than a Higher Power to you. He will be the God of your very life."

When you know that you know that God is who He says He is, you'll be infused with strength to walk with grace through situations that you never dreamed you'd be able to endure. When you know God and trust Him for whatever you need, you can relax and rely on His strength to be your strength and His peace to be your peace, in spite of whatever looms in front of you.

> Little faith will bring your souls to heaven, but great faith will bring heaven to your souls.[2]
>
> —CHARLES SPURGEON

I recently bumped into a good friend at the grocery store. This woman has faced many tough trials, including chronic illness and financial reversals, but she has a strong trust in the Lord. As we chatted about new developments in her life, she said, "I guess I should be worried about this latest mess, but I'm not! I trusted God a long time ago, and He's always come through, so what good would it do to worry now?" Great point! She knows He is all-powerful, all-knowing, and all-loving, so she's decided to trust what she knows and see what He does. After all, He is the Highest Power, and He is her life.

God Is Our Hiding Place

None of us can be certain what will happen in our lives from one day to the next, but we have the assurance that God is God and we can trust Him with our lives and with all that we care about. That knowledge provides a place of security, a hiding place for His children.

The following words from the psalmist are worth tucking away in your memory vault for anytime you need sweet comfort in the days ahead:

> You are my hiding place;
>> You shall preserve me from trouble;
>> You shall surround me with songs of deliverance. Selah
> I will instruct you and teach you in the way you should go;
>> I will guide you with My eye. (Ps. 32:7–8 NKJV)

That word *Selah* means "stop and think about this," and I believe that's excellent advice for the Smart Girl. I've found that God can indeed be trusted to preserve me from troubles—only if I will let Him! For example, I learned the hard way never to push open a door of opportunity on my own, because God already is working behind the scenes to open doors for my well-being and His glory.

I fell through a trapdoor several years ago after shoving open the wrong door. I was convinced that God had called me to enter into ministry with a friend. Despite a few reservations, I never considered whether or not this was really God's plan for me because it all came about so easily. It never occurred to me that I might be pushing open a door that I didn't need to walk through. I soon realized the mistake I'd made. Getting out of the situation was far more difficult than starting it up. I then went through a season of despair because I thought I'd blundered so badly that I'd never again have the opportunity to do some other things that I love so much.

God allowed me to go through a desert period, when fulfilling work seemed continually out of reach, but during that time He taught me some incredible lessons. I wrote my first book as a result of what I learned, and from that time on, He has opened doors and I've walked through them without pushing. Any time I'm tempted to rush ahead, I remember that God is working behind the scenes and my job is to relax, follow patiently where He leads, and let Him open the doors He chooses in His own way and in His own time.

God Speaks to Those Who Listen

Taking time to listen to God and to discern what He's calling us to do is a discipline we all can embrace. Sometimes in our great need to be heard we forget that listening allows God to be heard. I believe I've learned more in the silence, listening to Him, than I've ever learned as I prayed and begged Him for answers. At times I wasn't even asking the right questions, but when I quieted my mind and listened, really listened, I heard what I needed to hear.

Contemplative listening is a rich experience for those willing to make time to be still in God's presence. The Lord instructs us, "Be still, and know that I am God . . . " (Ps. 46:10). In the original Hebrew, the phrase *be still* means "cease striving" or "let go, relax." I know it's hard to shut out everything and immerse yourself in silence, but it can be done. As a starting point, set aside ten minutes and just be quiet. Turn off the music, the phone, and the television. Be quiet and invite God to speak to you in your spirit. As you grow comfortable with the silence and learn to hear God's voice, I think you'll want to set aside longer periods of time in which you deliberately listen for His counsel.

When I actually get quiet and listen, I find that God usually has something to tell me about myself—and often He points to something I need to think twice about. Sometimes when I think I have things all figured out, He reminds me that His ways are not my ways and His thoughts are far better than my best ideas. I also have noticed that regularly reading the Scriptures provides a deep well from which the Holy Spirit can draw wisdom to guide and instruct me in these quiet moments of intense listening.

Not long ago I was wondering what to do about a relationship that was a little askew. God reminded me in the quiet that "love covers a multitude of sins." That wasn't what I wanted to hear, but it was what I needed to hear. I had read many times the verse, "Above all, love each other deeply, because love covers over a multitude of sins" (1 Pet. 4:8 NIV), and although I understood the concept that "love covers," it wasn't until I needed that particular word for my own situation that it became alive and powerful in my life. I wouldn't have gone looking for that answer, but by pursuing silence, I had a chance to hear His wisdom over my preconceived ideas.

God Is Faithful—All the Time

Sometimes in the silence, God will bring to mind something I've witnessed in person or I've read in Scripture about His proven faithfulness in the past. This can give us strength and courage to face new trials. I think of the shepherd boy, David, rising up to fight the Philistine giant who had come against his countrymen and insulted his God, while Saul's soldiers hid themselves and wondered, "What will we do?"

> David said to Saul, "Don't let anyone be discouraged. I, your servant, will go and fight this Philistine!"
> Saul answered, "You can't go out against this Philistine and

fight him. You're only a boy. Goliath has been a warrior since he was a young man." (1 Sam. 17:32–33 NCV)

In reply David told Saul, in essence, "I have all the experience I need. When I was keeping my father's sheep, I killed lions and bears on a regular basis. What is this uncircumcised Philistine going to do that the lion and the bear couldn't do? He is taunting the armies of my God and I don't like it. The Lord saved me from the lion and the bear, and He'll do the same with this raging Philistine."

I can picture Saul shaking his head with dismay and not a little worry as he said, "Go, and may the LORD be with you" (1 Sam. 17:37 NCV).

Well, we know what happened next. David picked up five smooth stones, grabbed his slingshot and went out to meet Goliath. Since Goliath was over nine feet tall, I imagine that David could feel the earth move with every step the giant made toward him.

When Goliath looked at David and saw that he was only a boy, tanned and handsome, he looked down on David with disgust. He said, "Do you think I am a dog, that you come at me with a stick?" He used his gods' names to curse David. He said to David, "Come here. I'll feed your body to the birds of the air and the wild animals!"

But David said to him, "You come to me using a sword and two spears. But I come to you in the name of the LORD All-Powerful, the God of the armies of Israel! You have spoken against him. Today the LORD will hand you over to me, and I'll kill you and cut off your head. Today I'll feed the bodies of the Philistine soldiers to the birds of the air and the wild animals. Then all the world will know there is a God in Israel! Everyone gathered here will know the LORD does not need swords or spears to save people. The battle belongs to him, and he will hand you over to us." (1 Samuel 17:42–47 NCV)

Wow. Those were mighty big words for such a young man, but David knew who God was, he knew he could trust Him, and it was obvious that no one else was going to put an end to this menace. So David ran toward the giant, put one of his five stones into a sling, and let it fly.

His aim was true. The stone hit Goliath in the forehead, and the giant fell flat on his face.

> So David defeated the Philistine with only a sling and a stone. He hit him and killed him. He did not even have a sword in his hand. Then David ran and stood beside him. He took Goliath's sword out of its holder and killed him by cutting off his head. (1 Samuel 17:50–51 NCV)

I guess we can say of David, "no brag, just fact." He remembered his past record with God, he did what he said he was going to do, and his trust in God saved his neck one more time.

What about your record with God? In what ways has He rescued you in the past? How does your hindsight of God's faithfulness through past events provide assurance that He will enable you to more than survive whatever lies ahead?

One of the valuable hindsights I've gained that makes growing older a little less daunting is that I now have lived through the deaths of people I love. There was a time, before I had ever faced death, when I wondered how I would respond when it came. When loved ones began to die, the Lord was with me every time. He gave me a peace that passed understanding. It was as if He wrapped me in a grace bubble in each situation until I could get my bearings and keep going. He didn't remove the pain, nor did He remove the need for grieving. He walked alongside me through each situation and reassured me that He is in control, He cares, and He is faithful—all the time. I know that He will walk me through whatever comes in the years ahead because He is God and He has already proved faithful.

Go Forward, Confident in What You Know

When you know God—really know His character based on His Word, His past actions, and His promised intentions toward His people—you will be a strong, smart, settled woman of God. A verse in Daniel 11 sums it up in pretty powerful words: "The people who know their God shall be strong, and carry out great exploits." (v. 32 NKJV).

In fact, what you know and believe about God is the foundation of every decision you'll make. You may have a good head on your shoulders and certainly you draw on your intelligence and common sense for guidance when you Stop, Look, Listen, and Look Again, but a truly Smart Girl recognizes that all wisdom originates with and is given by God. "The fear of the LORD is the beginning of wisdom, and the knowledge of the Holy One is understanding" (Prov. 9:10 NKJV).

For all of our experience, logic, theories, and intelligence, there remains so very much we don't know and can't know as limited, finite human beings. Just about the time we figure out one situation, we're confronted with fresh questions from another direction. The best we can do when the answers aren't clear is to go with what we *do* know and rest in the fact that what we don't know is somehow wrapped up in the mystery of the God we trust. "God alone understands the way to wisdom; he knows where it can be found" (Job 28:23). We can rely on Him to show us ways we could never devise ourselves and answers we could never conceive on our own.

Smart Girls know that He is God. We are not.

In-Depth Study and Discussion Guide

Dearest Smart Girl,

You are a delight to my soul because you have chosen to Stop, Look, and Listen and maybe even to Look Again at some wonderful truths from God's Word. It is a good thing for us to know and understand that what God speaks to us, matters to us. I love the cheerfulness of these words from Psalm 119:

> Happy are those who live pure lives,
> who follow the LORD's teachings.
> Happy are those who keep his rules,
> who try to obey him with their whole heart. (vv. 1–2 NCV)

How encouraging! The word for *happy* means *blessed*. It is the joyful mental and spiritual contentment of following the words of God.

Smart Girls have figured out that to think on God's teaching is all good—there's nothing negative about it. So as you begin this Smart Girl Bible Study, please know you have my love, you have my prayers, and you are embarking on a sweet journey with the Lord.

What Do You Think? This first part of the study is for your personal meditation or for group discussion—either way will work with this study guide. Give yourself time to ponder the questions and candidly answer them. If you are meeting with a group, be honest but also be caring with one another. Everyone approaches Bible study from different experiences and diverse backgrounds, but, gratefully, when we are in Christ, we all share the same "Spirit of truth" who "will guide you into all truth" (John 16:13).

What Has God Said? This second part focuses on one or more Bible passages that emanate from the Smart Girl chapter you read. As you think through the questions, Stop, Look, Listen, and Look Again for what God is saying. He loves to speak to us, and His heart is made glad when we listen and obey. As you consider what God has said, I hope you will be encouraged to ask yourself, *how can I make what God says real in my life, right now?*

Let's get started!

Know you are loved,
Jan Silvious

P. S.
I'd love to hear from you when you graduate from Smart Girl School!

Chapter 1

Making Choices with Confidence

Smart Girls Think Twice About Consequences

What Do You Think?

1. Look back over your adult life and identify three of the most significant choices you have made.

2. What are some of the consequences of those choices in your life today?

3. Has someone else made important choices that have affected your life? What have been the consequences—good or bad?

What Has God Said?

1. Read Exodus 1:8–2:9. List the women you find in this passage.

2. List the choices and consequences for each one.

3. Were any of them in a position where they couldn't make a choice? Why or why not?

4. What was God's part in the consequences of their choices (both the stated and not stated)?

5. Read Romans 8:26–39. What do you discover in this passage that can give you confidence in making choices?

6. What do you think is the greatest fear you have about making a choice?

7. Is there a truth from this chapter's lesson that you can make your own when you are faced with choices? If so, what is *your* truth?

Lord, Thank You that You are waiting to hold me up with Your great love and kindness, not to trip me up in my choices. Help me to trust You, to understand Your leading instead of doubting You. Remind me, Lord, to see that Your loving kindness endures forever.

Chapter 2

For Real—It's a Warning!

Smart Girls Think Twice About Red Flags

What Do You Think?

1. List two or three situations in your life where there were some major red flags.

2. What was your response to the warnings? Did you stop when you saw them, or did you plow through them?

3. What happened as a result? What kind of an impact did this make in your own life or someone else's?

What Has God Said?

1. Read the following passages and see what God's red flags are about listening:

> Proverbs 5:1
> Proverbs 9:1–12
> Proverbs 10:16–17
> Proverbs 15:31–33
> Proverbs 19:20–21

2. What appears to be the cost of failing to pay attention to warnings? What is the benefit of listening?

3. Read the following account and note the red flags that surrounded Jesus' birth: Matthew 1:20, 2:1–21.

4. How serious do you believe God was about the red flags He posted? What would have happened if anyone had disobeyed at any point?

5. What are the red flags that are part of your world? Discuss how well you pay attention to them or how often you ignore them. What are the results?

6. How would you like to respond to the red flags you come up against? Is there something on the horizon right now that might be a red flag instead of a green light?

7. (Optional group discussion question) Think of a statement you can say to yourself when you come up against red flags—just a little attention getter, such as "If the flag looks red, you might be dead!" or "Think once and think again," or "Look twice—it saves money!"—whatever you might be able to come up with. Have fun with this exercise. It will help you remember how to spot red flags and will make for a good discussion.

Lord, give me eyes to see the red flags that You wave in front of me—about little things as well as big things. Give me an understanding heart and wisdom to see beyond my own reasoning. Thank You for being attentive to every detail of my life.

Chapter 3

Don't Let Life Slip Away

Smart Girls Think Twice About Time

What Do You Think?

1. Are you a *time* person or a *whenever* kind of girl? Do you think about your time as something to be managed, or do you go with *que será, será* (what will be, will be)?

2. What are some of the major time markers in your life? For instance, your birth date or anniversary, the day you accepted salvation, the birth of your first child, or when you broke a leg. Events have a way of marking time and creating seasons. Recall a significant experience that is a time marker in your life.

3. How would you describe your view of time? What influences in your life do you believe have determined your view of time? Take the time to discuss, if you are in a group, before moving on to the next section.

What Has God Said?

1. Read Ephesians 2 and mark the time phrases. These may be references to what has happened already, what is currently true, or what is still to come. Pay special attention to what things *were* (in the past tense) and what things *are* (in the present tense).

2. Read 1 Peter 2:9–10, and mark what is past and what is true for right now.

3. Why do you think *what was* and *what is* are important to God?

4. If God lives in eternity, why do you think He makes time references in Scripture?

5. Write out Psalm 1:3 in your own words. How would you define the season you're currently in? How is it different from other seasons you have experienced?

6. Where would you like to be in the next season of your life with God? Will that desire change the way you use your time? If so, how?

Father, I thank You that you say my times are in Your hands (Ps. 31:15). Keep me aware of the gift You have given me in the days, weeks, and months of my life. Make me a Smart Girl with my time on earth and keep eternity with You ever before me.

Chapter 4

Checks and Balances

Smart Girls Think Twice About Money

What Do You Think?

1. What is your relationship to money? How are you doing on the money management scale below? Mark where you see yourself.

1 2 3 4 5 6 7 8 9 10

Money manages me!   I manage my money.

2. Think about your own personal philosophy about money and how you use it. How would you explain this to someone else?

3. In what ways have you learned your biggest money lessons to date?

What Has God Said?

1. Read the following passage from Isaiah 55:1–3 (NASB), and ask yourself these questions:

> *What is God saying about life?*
> *What is He saying about money?*
> *What is He saying about Himself?*

> Ho! Every one who thirsts, come to the waters;
> And you who have no money come, buy and eat

> Come, buy wine and milk
> Without money and without cost.
> Why do you spend money for what is not bread,
> And your wages for what does not satisfy?
> Listen carefully to Me, and eat what is good,
> And delight yourself in abundance.
> Incline your ear and come to Me.
> Listen, that you may live.

2. Read John 10:9–10. What relationship do you see between this passage and Isaiah 55:1–3?

3. Spend a few extra minutes now reflecting on Matthew 6:31–34. What are the key principles in this passage? How do these truths affect your view of money?

4. Develop a Smart Girl statement about money that seems to sum up God's perspective on how you are to view and handle money. Write it out on a small card (credit card size!) and tuck it into your wallet where you can see it when you pull out cash or a credit card. Start your summary with "God says . . ." Also, ask God to remind you of *His* view of money.

Father, please keep me clear about money and its power and potential. Protect me from myself and any faulty thinking that causes me financial grief. Give me Your wisdom and open my heart to the way You want me to use the money You have given me. I specifically trust You for _____ (as it relates to money). I look forward to seeing how You answer.

Chapter 5

Is It True? Is It Kind? Is It Necessary?

Smart Girls Think Twice About Words

What Do You Think?

1. What are your favorite words to hear? How do you feel when you hear them?

2. What are your least favorite words to hear? How do you feel when you hear them?

3. Do you have a personal code for the kind of words you will speak? If so, what is it?

4. How do you think the people around you describe the way you speak? (I mean the people who are really close around you!)

What Has God Said?

1. Read the following verses and think about the many ways words can be used—for good or for ill:

> Proverbs 18:2, 4, 6–8, 13, 19–20, 23
> Proverbs 19:1, 5, 22, 25
> Proverbs 20:3, 15, 19, 20
> Proverbs 21:9, 19, 23
> Proverbs 22:11–13

2. What are some of your favorite *kind* words that God speaks to

you? What words does God use to describe His child in the following verses:

> Zephaniah 3:17
> Jeremiah 31:3
> Isaiah 49:16

3. How careful are you about the words you speak to yourself? (Remember, if you want to be wiser about the words you speak to yourself, it will require you to listen carefully to what you say and then to practice speaking kindly to yourself.)

4. List one unkind thing you say to yourself, such as *I'm so stupid!* or *I'm such a klutz!* With what words of kindness can you replace that unkind statement?

5. Choose one of the verses from question 2 and read it aloud to yourself several times, replacing *you* with *me*. Write it out on a sticky note and place it where you can see it every morning—ask God to open your heart to the wonderful words He says about *you*.

Father, thank You for loving me and for speaking kind words about me in the Scriptures. I love You and want to use my words to bless You. Help me to be aware of the times I forget to be loving with my words. I specifically want to bless _____ with my words this week and ask for the opportunity to do so.

Chapter 6

Relatively Speaking

Smart Girls Think Twice About Family

What Do You Think?

1. What comes to your mind when you hear the word *family*? Make a list of the words that come off the top of your head. (Be honest and don't edit!)

2. Since you have become an adult, what kind of family have you created around yourself? Does this family work for you? If not, how would you like to see it improved?

What Has God Said?

1. Read Genesis 2:18–4:25 and consider how important family might be in God's economy. Why did God make woman? What three acts made marriage, in God's eyes? (Gen. 2:24)

2. Describe the first couple's family. What is your impression of them?

3. Why do you think God didn't intervene and correct their issues when they came up?

4. Having read the Genesis passage, it's obvious that we all come from somewhere. Who is our mother?

5. Read Ephesians 2:18–19. In your heavenly family, who is your Father?

6. What do you see as your gift from your heavenly family? How does this affect you as a Smart Girl who loves God?

7. No matter what earthly family you came from and no matter who you have gathered around you, what is true about your heavenly family?

8. After reviewing this chapter and study, what are you feeling about your family of origin? What have been their gifts to you, both positive and negative? In the light of your heavenly family, how can you put your earthly family in perspective?

9. Are you more distant than you would like to be with one of the members of your earthly family? If so, why not take some time this week to call or send a note to bring about a little reconnection? Sometimes a small touch brings about a warm response. If that person doesn't respond, don't be offended, just wait a while and reach out again. In the meantime, pray for each member of your family, seeing each one with God's eyes and surrounding each with God's love.

Father, I am grateful for the people around me who make up what I call my family; rough edges and all, I love them. Thank You for being my Father no matter what comes along. Make me sensitive and kind in the old places where I might have become hard and calloused. Tenderize my heart with Your love.

Chapter 7

You've Gotta Love 'Em

Smart Girls Think Twice About Men

What Do You Think?

1. When you think about the differences between men and women, what do you believe are the most significant?

2. Take a minute to list at least three things you really like about honorable, decent men?

3. Can you quickly call to mind a couple of experiences with men that have formed your general response to the male species? Would you say you are generally positive or negative and why?

What Has God Said?

1. Have you ever thought about who determined whether you would live life as a male or a female? What do you learn from the following verses:

> Psalm 139:13–14
> Psalm 119:73
> Isaiah 44:24
> Job 10:11

2. Do you think God loves men and women equally? (Be honest!) Now look at Galatians 3:26–29. When it comes to the good news of the gospel, is there a difference between men and women?

3. Read Ephesians 5:22–33. What does God's heart seem to be toward men and women in this passage? Do you think His intent could be misunderstood? If so, why, and if not, why not?

4. Read the following passages that show Jesus' interaction with women. What do you learn from these encounters?

> John 4:7–28
> John 8:1–11
> John 11:17–33

5. Since Jesus walked among us to show us what the Father is like, how would you describe God's thoughts toward you as a woman?

6. If you have made mistakes in your relationships with men, where does that leave you in God's perspective? Can you write your own personal prayer that starts, "Lord, I know I have made mistakes with men, but I thank You that . . ."

7. Is there a man in your life to whom you owe an apology or an explanation of something you have said or done? If so, write a sentence about what you could possibly do.

8. Or would you like to send an affirming note to a man who has been a godly example? Take the time to do one of these actions. (Smart Girls don't just let relationships rock on without proper attention!)

Lord, thank You for Your love for me, for Your plans for me, and for Your care for me all the days of my life. Fill me with a sense of delight in the way that I am made and give me the grace to be the woman You intend for me to be.

Chapter 8

All the Good You Can Do

Smart Girls Think Twice About Living Generously

What Do You Think?

1. List several ways that another's generosity to you has touched your life.

2. How generous do you want to be? Write down some of the ways you would like to be more generous.

3. Does fear ever enter your thinking about generosity? If so, how does it affect you?

What Has God Said?

1. Read these wonderful words from 2 Corinthians 9:6–15 (NCV), a virtual gold mine of wisdom regarding giving. Pull out the gold for yourself as you look for the answers to the following questions:

> *How should you give?*
> *What is the attitude of a giver God loves?*
> *What is God's part in your giving?*
> *What does your giving do for God?*
>
> Remember this: The person who plants a little will have a small harvest, but the person who plants a lot will have a big harvest. Each of you should give as you have decided in your heart to give. You should not be sad

when you give, and you should not give because you feel forced to give. God loves the person who gives happily. And God can give you more blessings than you need. Then you will always have plenty of everything—enough to give to every good work. It is written in the Scriptures: "He gives freely to the poor. The things he does are right and will continue forever."—Psalm 112:9

God is the One who gives seed to the farmer and bread for food. He will give you all the seed you need and make it grow so there will be a great harvest from your goodness. He will make you rich in every way so that you can always give freely. And your giving through us will cause many to give thanks to God. This service you do not only helps the needs of God's people, it also brings many more thanks to God. It is a proof of your faith. Many people will praise God because you obey the Good News of Christ—the gospel you say you believe—and because you freely share with them and with all others. And when they pray, they will wish they could be with you because of the great grace that God has given you. Thanks be to God for his gift that is too wonderful for words.

2. How does this passage address the fear you identified earlier in the first part of this lesson?

3. In five minutes, list as many benefits to giving as you can.

4. We often equate generosity with financial giving. Do you know someone who is a generous giver in areas other than money? How is that person generous?

5. Write a two-or-three sentence description of a generous giver. Would someone else describe you this way?

6. Begin a little list of ways you can give to others that does not include money. Determine how you can follow through with your giving.

7. Complete this lesson with thanks to God for His gift to you as described in 2 Corinthians 9:15 as "too wonderful for words."

Lord, I am grateful for Your goodness to me which has surpassed anything I can imagine. I pray that You will make me a giver from the inside out! Make me aware of what I can give and to whom I can give—then give me the grace to do it!

Chapter 9

Give Yourself a Break
Smart Girls Think Twice About Rest

What Do You Think?

1. How do you feel when you are physically, mentally, and spiritually rested? (Use as many descriptive words as you can think of.)

2. How do you feel when you haven't rested? (Again, use descriptive words.)

3. What keeps you from a regular time of rest?

4. Have you ever really considered the significance of rest in your life? Explain.

What Has God Said?

1. Read the following scriptures and note the words that surround God's invitation to rest.

> Rest in the LORD and wait patiently for Him;
> Do not fret because of him who prospers in his way,
> Because of the man who carries out wicked schemes.
> Cease from anger and forsake wrath;
> Do not fret; it leads only to evildoing.—Psalm 37:7–8 NASB

> My soul, wait in silence for God only,
> For my hope is from Him.
> He only is my rock and my salvation,
> My stronghold; I shall not be shaken.—Psalm 62:5–6 NASB

2. What are the words that tell you the last passage is about *real* rest?

3. Spend a few extra minutes thinking about the following passage:

> LORD, my heart is not haughty,
> Nor my eyes lofty.
> Neither do I concern myself with great matters,
> Nor with things too profound for me.
> Surely I have calmed and quieted my soul,
> Like a weaned child with his mother;
> Like a weaned child is my soul within me.—Psalm 131:1–2 NKJV

4. From the Psalm 131 passage, list the instructions for quieting your soul.

5. What is the behavior of a weaned child? How does that behavior relate to rest?

6. You know your own lifestyle. What is your number one block to rest? Do you want to find a deeper rest in your life, and if so, what will it take to arrange for it?

7. How willing are you to consider making rest a higher priority in your life? Write your own prayer below, being honest about your struggles in this area along with your desire to experience more rest in your life.

Dear Lord, _____

_____

_____

_____

_____

_____

Chapter 10

Who Will You Trust with Your Life?

Smart Girls Think Twice About God

What Do You Think?

1. What are the first words that come to your mind when someone mentions the name of God?

2. If you had to introduce Him to someone, could you? If you think you could, what would you say?

3. What do you believe about God's power and goodness?

What Has God Said?

1. Read and think through the following scriptures. As you read each one, list the most notable fact about God.

> Genesis 18:14
> Deuteronomy 4:7–8
> Jeremiah 32:17, 27
> Zechariah 8:6–8
> Matthew 19:26
> Luke 1:37
> Romans 4:21

2. What do these scriptures tell you about God? Write a paragraph and include everything that you discovered, then

share your paragraph with the study group or with a friend. Tuck it away someplace where you can find it on a rainy day!

3. God tells us in His Word that we can know Him. How confident are you in your personal relationship with God?

4. Read the verses that follow. What do you learn about "knowing that you know" Him?

> 1 John 4:7
> Romans 8:16–17a

5. If you know that you are related to Him, list three of the gracious blessings you have in your life because of that relationship.

6. If you are not sure you have a relationship with God, now is a great time to tell Him that you know that you need Him. He is waiting to meet you right where you are. You might want to pray this prayer, and if you truly want to have a relationship with God, you will find Him waiting. Then share with someone in your group or a friend about this step!

God, I know I need you. I know I have fallen short of Your mark, and I understand that Jesus Christ has made me acceptable to You through His death on the cross and resurrection. I ask You to receive me, change me, direct my life, and get me safely home.

If you are already a believer, be intentional about praying for those you know who are seeking a relationship with God. There is nothing sweeter than having a friend join you on your journey with the Lord.

Notes

An Intelligent Attitude Toward Life

1. Paul Tillich, *Systematic Theology,* vol. I (Chicago, IL: University of Chicago Press, 1963), 51.
2. Spiros Zodhiates, ed. and comp., *The Hebrew-Greek Key Word Study Bible: New American Standard Bible* (Chattanooga, TN: AMG Publishers, 1984), 1725.
3. Dan Baker, *What Happy People Know* (New York: St Martin's Griffin, 2003), 135.
4. Jerry Sittser, *Discovering God's Will* (Grand Rapids, MI: Zondervan, 2000), 4.

Chapter 1

1. Denis Waitley, *Seeds of Greatness* (New York: Simon & Schuster Pocket Books, 1983), 87.
2. Gary Ryan Blair, *Everything Counts!* 2nd ed. (Tampa, FL: The GoalsGuy, 2006), 1.
3. This quote originated with Dr. Wayne A. Barber, senior teaching pastor at Hoffmantown Baptist Church, Albuquerque, New Mexico.
4. Gary Chapman, *The Four Seasons of Marriage* (Carol Stream, IL: Tyndale House Publishers, 2007).
5. This quote originated with Dr. Wayne A. Barber, senior teaching pastor at Hoffmantown Baptist Church, Albuquerque, New Mexico.

Notes

Chapter 2

1. Albert Schweitzer, quoted in *The Schweitzer Album* by Erica Anderson (New York: Harper & Row, 1965), 65.
2. Spiros Zodhiates, ed. and comp., *The Hebrew-Greek Key Word Study Bible: New American Standard Bible* (Chattanooga, TN: AMG Publishers, 1984), 1777.
3. William Shakespeare, *All's Well that Ends Well*, Act iii, Scene 5.

Chapter 3

1. Dale Carnegie, *How to Stop Worrying and Start Living* (New York: Simon & Schuster Pocket Books, 1985), 11.
2. *The Columbia World of Quotations* citing Leslie Halliwell, *Halliwell's Filmgoer's Companion* (New York: Columbia University Press, 1984).
3. Max Lucado, *He Still Moves Stones* (Dallas, TX: Word Publishing, 1993), 91.

Chapter 4

1. Ralph Earle, *Word Meanings in the New Testament* (Peabody, MA: Hendrickson Publishers, 2005), 7.
2. Pat Regnier and Amanda Gengler, "Men, Women . . . and Money," *Money* Magazine, March 14, 2006, www.money.cnn.com/2006/ 03/10/pf/marriagemain_moneymag_0604/index.htm.
3. Billy Graham, *Hope for Each Day* (Nashville, TN: J. Countryman, 2002), 81.

Chapter 5

1. Charles R. Swindoll, *Swindoll's Ultimate Book of Illustrations and Quotes* (Nashville, TN: Thomas Nelson, 1998), 38.

Chapter 6

1. Gail Lumet Buckley, *The Hornes: An American Family* (New York: Alfred A. Knopf, 1986), 4.
2. Robert Frost, "The Death of a Hired Man," *North of Boston* (New York: Henry Holt and Company, 1915; Bartleby.com, 1999); www.bartleby.com/118.
3. Jane Howard, *Families* (New York: Simon & Schuster, 1978).
4. Maurice Seitter, quoted in *Saving Your Second Marriage Before It Starts* by Les and Leslie Parrott (Grand Rapids, MI: Zondervan, 1995, 2006), 24.
5. Ralph Ellison, quoted in "Ovid in Ossining," *Time*, March 27, 1964.

Notes

Chapter 7

1. Anne Moir and David Jessel, *Brain Sex* (New York: Random House, 1989, 1991), 70.
2. George Santayana, *The Life of Reason: The Phases of Human Progress* (New York: Scribner, 1906).
3. Moir and Jessel, Ibid., 56.
4. Helen Rowland, *A Guide to Men* (New York: Dodge Publishing, 1922).
5. Jean Kerr, *The Snake Has All the Lines* (New York: Doubleday & Company, Inc., 1960).
6. Marlene Dietrich, *Marlene Dietrich's ABC* (New York: Doubleday & Company, Inc., 1961).

Chapter 8

1. Henry Drummond, *The Greatest Thing in the World* (Chicago: Moody, 1884; Bridge-Logos, 2001 reprint), 37.
2. William Barclay, *The Gospel of Luke* (Philadelphia, PA: The Westminster Press, 1953), 76.

Chapter 9

1. E. K. Chambers, comp., *The Oxford Book of Sixteenth Century Verse* (Oxford: Oxford University Press, 1932).
2. Daniel G. Amen, *Making a Good Brain Great* (New York: Random House, 2005), 86–87.
3. Ibid.
4. Edna St. Vincent Millay, "First Fig," *A Few Figs from Thistles* (New York: Harper, 1922), 9.
5. Mason Cooley, *City Aphorisms* (New York: Eleventh Selection, 1993).
6. Dan Baker, *What Happy People Know* (New York: St Martin's Griffin, 2003), 81.
7. Frederick Buechner, *Listening to Your Life* (New York: HarperCollins, 1992), 289.

Chapter 10

1. John Piper, *The Pleasures of God* (Colorado Springs, CO: Multnomah Publishers, 1991), 193.
2. Charles Haddon Spurgeon, quoted in *Spurgeon on Leadership* by Larry J. Michael, 3rd ed. (Grand Rapids, MI: Kregel Publications, 2003), 186–187.

An irresistible invitation to discover the fun and freedom of living as a big girl.

Every little girl wants to be a big girl.

But once we've grown up and life becomes stressful, it's easy to revert to Little-Girl behaviors: pouting, neediness, manipulation, and even whining. Half of the time, we don't realize that we're doing it. Women who cling to Little-Girl ways miss out on the joys of being the confident, productive women whom God intends us to be.

Jan uses down-to-earth practicality and biblical wisdom to give us that encouraging nudge we need in order to:

- Resolve conflict peacefully—even if it means creating a crisis
- Handle wisely and truly enjoy our closest relationships
- Live more comfortably with our roles and responsibilities
- Build a legacy of strength and graciousness for the little girls who follow

Big Girls Don't Whine also includes a reader's guide for personal reflection and group discussion.

WOMEN of FAITH
INFINITE GRACE
CONFERENCE 2008

RELAX! Join us and learn why you can stop trying so hard. Come and see what it can mean to rest in God's amazing, unequaled, Infinite Grace!

Featuring the Women of Faith Team

PRE-CONFERENCE

Friday 9:00 AM - 3:00 PM
I Second That Emotion
Do your feelings have you tied in knots? You're not the only one! Join Patsy Clairmont, Anita Renfroe, and Jan Silvious for a day of laughter therapy and solid biblical teaching on understanding your emotions.

Coming to a City near YOU!

National Conference San Antonio, TX February 7 - 9	St. Louis, MO June 13 - 14	Kansas City, MO August 8 - 9	Portland, OR October 10 - 11
Omaha, NE March 28 - 29	East Rutherford, NJ June 20 - 21	Tampa, FL August 15 - 16	St. Paul, MN October 17 - 18
Little Rock, AR April 4 - 5	Seattle, WA June 27 - 28	Dallas, TX August 22 - 23	Houston, TX October 24 - 25
Fresno, CA April 11 - 12	Alaska Cruise Seattle, WA – Port City June 29 - July 6	Anaheim, CA September 5 - 6	Greensboro, NC October 31 - November 1
Spokane, WA April 18 - 19		Philadelphia, PA September 12 - 13	Ft. Lauderdale, FL November 7 - 8
Columbus, OH April 25 - 26	Washington, DC July 11 - 12	Denver, CO September 19 - 20	Oklahoma City, OK November 14 - 15
Jacksonville, FL May 16 - 17	Cleveland, OH July 18 - 19	Atlanta, GA September 26 - 27	Phoenix (Glendale), AZ November 21 - 22
Rochester, NY June 6 - 7	Boston, MA July 25 - 26	San Jose, CA October 3 - 4	
	Indianapolis, IN August 1 - 2		

"AND GOD IS ABLE TO MAKE ALL GRACE ABOUND TO YOU, THAT ALWAYS HAVING ALL SUFFICIENCY IN EVERYTHING, YOU MAY HAVE AN ABUNDANCE FOR EVERY GOOD DEED."
– II CORINTHIANS 9:8

Register NOW! Visit us at womenoffaith.com or call 888-49-FAITH

Dates, locations and speakers are subject to change. See registration deadlines at womenoffaith.com.